M000209872

THE MISS FIRECRACKER CONTEST

A PLAY

BY BETH HENLEY

**DRAMATISTS
PLAY SERVICE
INC.**

THE MISS FIRECRACKER CONTEST
Copyright © 1985, Beth Henley

All Rights Reserved

CAUTION: Professionals and amateurs are hereby warned that performance of THE MISS FIRECRACKER CONTEST is subject to payment of a royalty. It is fully protected under the copyright laws of the United States of America, and of all countries covered by the International Copyright Union (including the Dominion of Canada and the rest of the British Commonwealth), and of all countries covered by the Pan-American Copyright Convention, the Universal Copyright Convention, the Berne Convention, and of all countries with which the United States has reciprocal copyright relations. All rights, including professional/amateur stage rights, motion picture, recitation, lecturing, public reading, radio broadcasting, television, video or sound recording, all other forms of mechanical or electronic reproduction, such as CD-ROM, CD-I, DVD, information storage and retrieval systems and photocopying, and the rights of translation into foreign languages, are strictly reserved. Particular emphasis is placed upon the matter of readings, permission for which must be secured from the Author's agent in writing.

The stage performance rights in THE MISS FIRECRACKER CONTEST (other than first class rights) are controlled exclusively by DRAMATISTS PLAY SERVICE, INC., 440 Park Avenue South, New York, NY 10016. No professional or nonprofessional performance of the Play (excluding first class professional performance) may be given without obtaining in advance the written permission of DRAMATISTS PLAY SERVICE, INC., and paying the requisite fee.

Inquiries concerning all other rights should be addressed to The Gersh Agency, 130 West 42nd Street, New York, NY 10036. Attn: Peter Hagan.

SPECIAL NOTE

Anyone receiving permission to produce THE MISS FIRECRACKER CONTEST is required to give credit to the Author as sole and exclusive Author of the Play on the title page of all programs distributed in connection with performances of the Play and in all instances in which the title of the Play appears for purposes of advertising, publicizing or otherwise exploiting the Play and/or a production thereof. The name of the Author must appear on a separate line, in which no other name appears, immediately beneath the title and in size of type equal to 50% of the size of the largest, most prominent letter used for the title of the Play. No person, firm or entity may receive credit larger or more prominent than that accorded the Author. The following acknowledgment must appear on the title page in all programs distributed in connection with performances of the Play:

New York Premiere by the Manhattan Theatre Club on May 1, 1984.

THE MISS FIRECRACKER CONTEST was presented by the Manhattan Theatre Club, in New York City, on May 1, 1984. It was directed by Stephen Tobolowsky; the scenery was designed by John Lee Beatty; the costumes were designed by Jennifer Von Mayrhauser; the lighting was designed by Dennis Parichy; the sound was designed by Stan Metelits; and the production stage manager was Wendy Chapin. The cast was as follows:

CARNELLE SCOTT .... Holly Hunter
POPEYE JACKSON .... Belita Moreno
ELAIN RUTLEDGE .... Patricia Richardson
DELMOUNT WILLIAMS .... Mark Linn-Baker
MAC SAM .... Budge Threlkeld
TESSY MAHONEY .... Margo Martindale

THE CAST

CARNELLE SCOTT, 24, the beauty contestant
POPEYE JACKSON, 23, Carnelle's seamstress
ELAIN RUTLEDGE, 32, Carnelle's first cousin; a beauty
DELMOUNT WILLIAMS, 28, Carnelle's first cousin;
  Elain's brother
MAC SAM, 36, the balloon man
TESSY MAHONEY, 23, the beauty contest coordinator

THE SETTING

The action of the play takes place in Brookhaven, Mississippi; a small southern town.

THE TIME

The ending of June and the beginning of July.

AUTHOR'S NOTE: It is strongly suggested that the actress playing Carnelle dye her hair bright red instead of opting for a wig.

SYNOPSIS OF SCENES

SCENE ONE: The living room of Ronelle William's house in Brookhaven, Mississippi — about five o'clock Monday afternoon on a hot day at the end of June.

There is something dreary and suffocating and frightening about the room with its dark oak furniture, its heavy, bright curtains and the endless clutter of nicknacks. An old spinning wheel sits in a far corner of the room.

There are three entrances and exits; a front door; a door leading to the kitchen; and a staircase leading to the upstairs rooms.

SCENE TWO: The same setting. About eight o'clock in the evening, on the following Saturday.

WITH LOVE AND STARS
TO STEPHEN

props: measuring tape
magnifying lense
crackers & tea
pictures - one of godlooking

THE MISS FIRECRACKER CONTEST

ACT I

SCENE ONE

The lights go up onstage. Carnelle Scott, 24, stands with her back to the audience looking into a mirror. Carnelle is tallish with an oddly attractive face, a nice figure and very bright dyed red hair. She wears purple leotards, tights and tap shoes.
Carnelle turns away from the mirror with a glint in her eyes. She pushes the rolled up rug back even further, then rushes to place the needle back on the record spinning on the record player. A sung version of "The Star Spangled Banner" begins playing loudly.
Carnelle checks a notebook, then rushes madly back to the kitchen. She quickly returns with wooden spoons and stainless steel knives. She leaps into her talent routine that requires tap dancing, marching and baton twirling, none of which she is extremely adept at. When the record comes to, "And the rockets red glare . . . " she picks up a wooden spoon that she uses as an imaginary roman candle. She says, "Pow," each time she imagines it goes off. For the final, "Oh, say does that . . ." she puts down the spoons and picks up two knives that she uses as imaginary sparklers. She twirls them about. When the record is over Carnelle goes to remove the needle, as she repeats part of her routine to herself.

CARNELLE. Let's see, that was, "And the rockets red glare — (*Then as the imaginary Roman candle goes off.*) Boom! — The bombs bursting in air — Boom! — gave proof — Boom! — through the night — Boom! — that our flag was — Boom! — there — Boom! Boom! Boom!" (*She goes to mark down the ideas in her notebook.*)

7

Hmm. I don't know. I think that'll work. I think it will. (*There is a knock on the door.*) Coming. Coming—! Coming! (*Before going to the door Carnelle shakes her head of red hair back and forth, takes a towel from a chair and slings it carelessly around her neck. She begins panting deeply as she goes to open the door for Popeye Jackson. Popeye, 23, is a small, glowing person. She wears a homemade dress with many different size pockets and thick glasses with heavy black rims. She does not carry a purse.*) Oh, hello, Popeye. Come in. Come on in.

POPEYE. Thanks.

CARNELLE. (*Still breathing heavily.*) Wheew! Just make yourself at home. Oh, and please excuse the way I look, but I've been practicing my routine. It's something, I tell you, hard work. But it's coming along. It's coming right along.

POPEYE. Good.

CARNELLE. (*After an awkward moment.*) Well. I guess what I should do is show you the sketches so you'll have some idea of what I want.

POPEYE. Alright.

CARNELLE. (*Getting the sketches.*) They're right over here, I believe. Yes, here they are. (*Turning around.*) What's that thing?

POPEYE. (*Who has removed a magnifying glass from her pocket.*) It's my magnifying lens.

CARNELLE. A magnifying lens? You need that thing to see with?

POPEYE. Well, up close I do.

CARNELLE. Goodness gracious. Well, here're the sketches. Of course, now, I'm not an artist or anything; so the drawings aren't much. (*Pause.*) But I think you'll get the general idea.

POPEYE. (*Looking at the sketches through the lens.*) Oh, that's pretty.

CARNELLE. (*As if someone has given her a gift.*) You think so?

POPEYE. I like them stars.

CARNELLE. Well, I wanted to go with something really patriotic. Kinda traditional. You know, noble, in a sense.

POPEYE. And this costume's for a dance contest?

CARNELLE. Well, no; it's not a dance contest; it's for the Miss Firecracker Contest.

POPEYE. (*In the dark.*) Huh?

CARNELLE. The Miss Firecracker Contest? (*Popeye shakes her head.*) It's the beauty contest. They have it in Brookhaven every

8

Fourth of July. It's a tradition. It's a big event. It's famous. Why Representative Louis Pooley's gonna be here this very year to put the crown on the winner's head. It's a famous contest.

POPEYE. Well, I guess, I just don't know nothing about it.

CARNELLE. Well, it's odd to me. It's really odd to me.

POPEYE. Course I haven't been here in town but a short while. Only 'bout three weeks.

CARNELLE. (*Relieved.*) Oh! Oh, well, that explains it! that explains it all!!

POPEYE. Yeah.

CARNELLE. Anyway, this outfit is what I'm gonna be wearing in the talent section of the contest.

POPEYE. Oh.

CARNELLE. What I do's kind of a tap-dance-march-type-a-thing. It's gonna be done to, "The Star Spangled Banner." I'm gonna end up spinning these lit up sparklers around and around—one in each hand. (*She twirls the imaginary sparklers.*)

POPEYE. Gosh!

CARNELLE. And before that Roman candles going off—(*As she shoots off imaginary roman candles.*) Boom! Boom! Boom! Like that—right out over the top a the crowd!

POPEYE. Really?

CARNELLE. Oh, sure.

POPEYE. Boy.

CARNELLE. Well, so you think you'll be able to make up a pattern following these drawings?

POPEYE. I expect so.

CARNELLE. Well, then . . . the job is yours.

POPEYE. Thank you.

CARNELLE. You're welcome.

POPEYE. Maybe I should go on and get your measurements off you right now if ya don't mind.

CARNELLE. Oh, no, no. Fine. Go ahead. All right.

POPEYE. (*Getting her measuring tape from her pocket.*) I just need a few.

CARNELLE. Take all you want. I'll just stand right here. (*She strikes a dramatic pose.*) Just natural. Is this okay with you? This stance right here?

POPEYE. Sure. (*She begins measuring, looking at the measurement through her glass, writing it down, then starting a new measurement.*)

CARNELLE. My, I feel like a model or something. Very elegant. Of course, that's exactly what I should be doing. Modeling, that is. People have told me that. They say, "Carnelle, why do you keep slaving away at Slater's Jewelry Shop? You should be up in Memphis working as a model. You really should."

POPEYE. (*Trying to get Carnelle to relax her tightly tucked in stomach.*) You can just relax.

CARNELLE. What? Oh, I'm fine. Just fine.

POPEYE. Alright. (*She finishes with the waist measurement, looks at it through the glass, writes it down, then goes on.*)

CARNELLE. You know you do this very well. Expertly, in fact. Of course, you come highly recommended to me from Miss Celia Lily. She says you've done some really fine work in her shop. She says you seem really experienced to her.

POPEYE. Well, I'm that for sure. See, I been making clothes practically all my life. Started out when I was four years old.

CARNELLE. Oh, really?

POPEYE. Used to make little outfits for the bullfrogs that lived out around our yard.

CARNELLE. Bullfrogs! Yuk!

POPEYE. They was funny looking creatures.

CARNELLE. But why didn't you design clothes for your dolls?

POPEYE. We din't have no dolls.

CARNELLE. Oh; how sad.

POPEYE. Them frogs was okay.

CARNELLE. But what kind of clothes could you design for a frog? They'd look ugly in anything.

POPEYE. Well . . . one thing was a nurse's suit. Oh, and I remember a queen's robe and a cape of leaves. Different things.

CARNELLE. (*With a giggle.*) Well, I certainly hope you don't think of me as any bullfrog.

POPEYE. Huh?

CARNELLE. I mean, think I'm ugly like one of those dumb bullfrogs of yours.

POPEYE. Oh, I don't.

CARNELLE. Well, of course, you don't. I was just joking.

POPEYE. Oh.

CARNELLE. (*Suddenly very sad and uncomfortable.*) Are you about done?

10

POPEYE. Mostly. This here's all I need. (*Carnelle stares forlornly into space as Popeye measures her head.*) There. Done.

CARNELLE. Well, I've got to stretch a minute. (*She stretches from her waist, then kicks her leg up high.*) There! And, kick! And . . . kick!

POPEYE. You sure do kick high!

CARNELLE. Well, I work at it daily.

POPEYE. I could never kick like that.

CARNELLE. I don't know, maybe you could with practice. Want to try it? Come on and try it. Go ahead! And kick! And kick! And kick! And kick! (*Popeye kicks feebly in the air.*) Not bad. Keep on working at it. That's the only way to improve. Listen, I have a snack made up for us in the kitchen. Would you like it now?

POPEYE. Sure.

CARNELLE. I hope you don't mind, it's just ice tea and saltine crackers.

POPEYE. I love saltines.

CARNELLE. Alright then, I'll go get the snack. (*Carnelle exits to the kitchen. Popeye looks around. She goes over to the spinning wheel and spins it around. She watches it. She pretends to prick her finger on the needle. Carnelle comes back in carrying the snack tray. She now has an apron on over her leotards. Popeye turns around startled.*)

POPEYE. This sure is a scary house.

CARNELLE. You don't like it?

POPEYE. It's scary.

CARNELLE. Well, it's just like my Aunt Ronelle fixed it up. It's got her special touch: this old spinning wheel; these lace doilies; these old pictures in frames here. I'd prefer something more modern and luxurious, but—that's just me.

POPEYE. You live here with your aunt?

CARNELLE. Oh, no. She died. She had cancer.

POPEYE. I'm sorry.

CARNELLE. It happened just a few weeks before last Christmas. We were very close. It was a tragedy.

POPEYE. I'm sorry.

CARNELLE. (*As she pours Popeye's tea.*) You may of heard about her; Ronnelle Williams? It was a famous medical case—ran in all the newspapers.

POPEYE. No.

CARNELLE. Well, see what it was—Do you take lemon?

POPEYE. Please.

CARNELLE. Anyway, she had this cancer of the pituitary gland, I believe it was; so what they did was they replaced her gland with the gland of a monkey to see if they could save her life—Just help yourself to the sugar—

POPEYE. (*Moving to sit on the floor.*) Thanks.

CARNELLE. And they did, in fact, keep her alive for a month or so longer than she was expected to live.

POPEYE. Well, that's good.

CARNELLE. (*Pouring herself some tea.*) Of course, there were such dreadful side effects.

POPEYE. Mmm.

CARNELLE. She, well, she started growing long, black hairs all over her body just, well, just like an ape.

POPEYE. Gracious, Lord.

CARNELLE. It was very trying. But she was so brave. She even let them take photographs of her. Everyone said she was just a saint. A saint or an angel; one or the other.

POPEYE. It gives me the shivers.

CARNELLE. It was awfully hard on me losing my Aunt Ronelle—although I guess I should be used to it by now.

POPEYE. What's that?

CARNELLE. People dying. It seems like people'v been dying practically all my life, in one way or another. First my mother passed when I was barely a year old. Then my Daddy kinda drug me around with him till I was about nine and he couldn't stand me any longer; so he dropped me off to live with my Aunt Ronelle and Uncle George and their own two children: Elain and Delmount. They're incredible those two. They're just my ideal. Anyhow, we're happy up until the time when Uncle George falls to his death trying to pull this bird's nest out from the chimney.

POPEYE. He fall off from the roof?

CARNELLE. That's right. Tommy Turner was passing by throwing the evening paper and he caught sight of the whole event. Boom.

POPEYE. How awful.

CARNELLE. Anyhow, my original Daddy appears back here to live with us looking all kinda fat and swollen. And after staying on with us about two years, he suddenly drops dead in the summer's heat while running out to the Tropical Ice Cream truck. Heart failure, they said it was. Then this thing with Aunt Ronelle dying right before Christmas. It's been hard to bear.

POPEYE. (*After a moment.*) I had a brother who was bit by a water moccasin down by the Pearl River, and he died.

CARNELLE. Well; you know, they say everyone's gonna be dying someday. I believe it to.

POPEYE. Yeah. May as well. (*She finishes a cracker and wipes her lips with a napkin.*) That sure was tasty.

CARNELLE. Well . . . thank you much. Would you like to see the material I've chosen to make my costume with?

POPEYE. Why, yes.

CARNELLE. Good. Then I'll just run get it.

POPEYE. Oh, Carnelle?

CARNELLE. Yes?

POPEYE. Do you mind if I look at these pictures in frames here?

CARNELLE. Oh, no. That's what they're there for. (*Carnelle exits upstairs to the bedrooms. Popeye goes over and picks up her magnifying glass. She then goes and looks at the pictures. She looks at one, then another, then suddenly, at the third picture, she is struck. She picks it up and looks at it, studying it closely with her lens.*)

POPEYE. My. Oh, my. (*Carnelle comes back down carrying a sack.*)

CARNELLE. Who are you looking at?

POPEYE. A man. This man here.

CARNELLE. Oh, that's my cousin, Delmount.

POPEYE. What eyes. Look at his hair — It's wild wouldn't you say? It's wild.

CARNELLE. Well, I suppose, Delmount is rather a romantic figure.

POPEYE. Really?

CARNELLE. He was always writing sheets and sheets of poetry to the women he loved then he'd set them all afire and bury the ashes.

POPEYE. (*Swooning.*) How sad!

CARNELLE. Yes, Delmount's very odd. He can do this trick where he wiggles his ears.

POPEYE. (*Totally sold that this is the man for her.*) He can!?

13

CARNELLE. Sure.

POPEYE. (*Impulsively.*) Where's he live now?

CARNELLE. Well, it's strange . . . see, Delmount, he's had kind of a checkered past.

POPEYE. Checkered?

CARNELLE. Right. And about the first of the year a Louisiana judge sentenced him to a—well, to a mental institution.

POPEYE. Is he mad?

CARNELLE. No. Not really. He hit a man in the face with a bottle; so his lawyer got him put there instead of jail.

POPEYE. Oh.

CARNELLE. (*Upset.*) He was released in the spring, but he hasn't been home since. I don't know where he is now.

POPEYE. I hope he's alright.

CARNELLE. Here, let's look at the material.

POPEYE. Alright.

CARNELLE. (*Taking the red material from the sack.*) Here's the red.

POPEYE. Ooooh, that's pretty. (*Touching it.*) Silky too.

CARNELLE. And, of course, the blue.

POPEYE. (*Looking at the material through her glass.*) It's just like a midnight sky. I love blue.

CARNELLE. And then, the most expensive, the most elegant of all—silver for the stars.

POPEYE. Why, you went all out on this material—I can see that.

CARNELLE. Well, yes. I hope it's gonna be okay. Not having any white. I mean, I hope red, blue and silver will be patriotic enough.

POPEYE. Well, I just can't wait to—

ELAIN'S VOICE. Carnelle! Carnelle, Honey! (*Elain Rutledge, 32, enters through the front door. She is dressed in elegant pastels but appears somewhat wilted in the summer's heat. Elain could most definitely be described as beautiful, but her looks are now more strained and anxious than they once were. She carries expensive luggage, a cosmetic case, and a gift.*)

CARNELLE. (*Running to hug her.*) Elain!! It's Elain!!!

ELAIN. (*Hugging her.*) Why, hello, my little Carnation! How are you doing?!

CARNELLE. (*Overlapping.*) Oh, Elain! Elain! I'm just fine!

14

ELAIN. Why, you really did dye your hair, didn't you?

CARNELLE. Do you like it?

ELAIN. Well, it's just as red as it can be!

CARNELLE. That's what I wanted, crimson red.

ELAIN. Well, then, it couldn't be more perfect! Will you help me with these bags, here? My arms are just falling off!

CARNELLE. (*Taking the biggest bags.*) Of course! I'm sorry! Goodness, I thought you weren't coming in till the weekend.

ELAIN. Oh, I know, I know. I suddenly decided to cut my stay off short with my mother-in-law. I decided just to drive by Hollybluff and beep twice.

CARNELLE. (*With a giggle.*) Oh, you crazy thing!

ELAIN. No, really, I'm sorry, dar'lin, I should a called you up but—(*Suddenly noticing Popeye.*) Why, hello, Honey!

CARNELLE. Oh, this is my friend, Popeye Jackson. Popeye, this is my cousin, Elain Rutledge, the one I—

ELAIN. (*Overlapping.*) Why, hello, Popeye, so nice to meet you. What a smashing outfit!

POPEYE. Thank you.

CARNELLE. Elain knows everything about clothes. She just adores them.

ELAIN. Oh you crazy dear! Look here's a little something I picked up for you at a shop in the Quarter. (*Handing Carnelle a gift.*)

CARNELLE. What! Oh, you shouldn't have! Really, you shouldn't have. (*She opens the box and takes out a very strangely decorated Mardi gras mask.*) Why look! It's beautiful! Isn't that beautiful!

ELAIN. I just thought of you when I saw it. You'll have to wear it to a mask ball.

CARNELLE. (*Holding the mask in front of her face.*) How elegant! How simply elegant! Look, Popeye!

POPEYE. May I hold it too?

CARNELLE. Why, of course. (*She hands Popeye the mask. Elain and Carnelle hug then turn back to Popeye. There is a moment of silence as Popeye holds the mask over her eyes and slowly moves her head from side to side. Perhaps she makes a strange sound.*)

ELAIN. (*Taking off her dangling, shimmering earrings and handing them out to Popeye.*) Oh, here, Popeye, these are for you.

POPEYE. What?

15

ELAIN. Please, they're a gift to you. Here, put them on.

POPEYE. Oh, no.

CARNELLE. Oh, Elain! Elain!

ELAIN. (*Overlapping.*) Yes, yes! I insist! They're just right for you; they're just your color. Here, I'll put them on for you. (*She puts the earrings on Popeye.*) Oh, stunning! They look just simply stunning!

POPEYE. (*Slowly shaking her head back and forth.*) Why, thank you.

CARNELLE. Isn't she wonderful, Popeye! Isn't she just perfectly perfect!

ELAIN. Oh, how I wish I were!

CARNELLE. Don't be silly; you are!

POPEYE. (*Shaking her head.*) I never had me no earbobs.

ELAIN. Well, I'm glad you have them, Popeye. They look dazzling on you.

POPEYE. Well. I think I better be going. It's getting towards dark. Let me get all this rounded up. (*She starts getting the materials together.*)

CARNELLE. Popeye's going to be using this material to make my costume for the Miss Firecracker Contest.

ELAIN. You mean, you went on and signed up for that?

CARNELLE. Yes, I registered today.

ELAIN. I don't see why you're so interested in being Miss Firecracker; there's nothing to it.

CARNELLE. Well, not for you. See, Elain was Miss Firecracker way back when she was just eighteen.

ELAIN. Well, seventeen, actually.

CARNELLE. Anyway, it was way back that first year when I came to live with them. She was a vision of beauty riding on that float with a crown on her head waving to everyone. I thought I'd drop dead when she passed by me.

ELAIN. All that was ages ago. It's silly to think about.

CARNELLE. Anyway, I just thought I'd give it a whirl. I'm twenty-four. Twenty-five's the age limit. I just thought I'd give it a whirl while I still could.

ELAIN. (*Powdering her nose.*) They ought to change that name to—well, to something like, Miss Fourth of July. Miss Firecracker sounds so trashy.

16

CARNELLE. Course, I don't expect to win — that's crazy. I'm just in it for the experience — that's the main thing.

POPEYE. Well, I think you'd be perfect for a Miss Firecracker — with your red hair and all.

CARNELLE. Oh, well, that's actually why I dyed my hair red; I thought it'd be more appropriate for the contest.

POPEYE. It's a nice dye job too. I don't see no roots or nothing.

CARNELLE. I try to do a careful job on it.

POPEYE. Well, I got it all together here.

CARNELLE. Good, well here're the sketches.

POPEYE. And when will you be needing your costume by?

CARNELLE. Oh. Well, the audition'll be this very Saturday; so could you have it by Wednesday afternoon or Thursday at the latest?

POPEYE. Tuesday's fine.

CARNELLE. Alright, I'll see you on Tuesday. (*Carnelle and Popeye are at the front door now.*)

POPEYE. Alright. Bye.

CARNELLE. Bye, bye.

POPEYE. (*To Elain.*) And I love my earbobs!

ELAIN. (*From the sofa.*) Oh, good!

POPEYE. Well, alright, bye. (*She exits.*)

CARNELLE. Bye, bye. (*Turning and coming back to Elain.*) Oh, Elain! That was so sweet what you did — giving Popeye those earrings. It meant so much to her. You're so generous!

ELAIN. (*Meaning it.*) Don't talk about it, please. It was nothing. Oh, mind if I have a glass of this delicious looking ice tea? I'm about ready to drop dead from the heat.

CARNELLE. Oh, of course! Please! Here, I'll run get you a fresh glass out from the kitchen. (*Carnelle picks up the tray and exits. Elain takes off her hat and fans herself. She looks sadly around the room. Carnelle returns with a glass with a small umbrella in it.*) Here, now —

ELAIN. Bless you.

CARNELLE. There you are.

ELAIN. Why, Carnation, you're saving my life. This is heaven. Sheer heaven!

CARNELLE. (*Running to Elain's clothes bag.*) Oh, Elain, did you bring that dress along with you that I asked about on the phone?

You know, the beautiful red antebellum dress that you wore at the Natchez Pilgrimage the first year you got married. See, it's gonna be perfect for me to wear in the contest. I'm trying to make crimson red my thematic color. (*Opening the bag: she discovers the dress is not there.*)

ELAIN. I see—but I thought you said you weren't gonna be needing a formal dress for the audition this Saturday.

CARNELLE. I know, that's true. We'll just need them in the actual contest for the opening Parade of Firecrackers.

ELAIN. So, why don't we just wait till after the audition and see if you make it to the pageant.

CARNELLE. Why? Don't you think I'll make it?

ELAIN. Well, I hope so, Carnelle, but they only pick five girls.

CARNELLE. Well . . . I've thought about it, and I, frankly, can't think of five other girls in town that are prettier than me. I'm speaking honestly now. Course I know there's Caroline Jeffers, but she has those yellow teeth—

ELAIN. (*Not wanting to get into it.*) My this mint is delicious! Did you grow it yourself?

CARNELLE. Aunt Ronelle planted it before she died.

ELAIN. Well, it's quite refreshing.

CARNELLE. I know why you're worried. You think I've ruined my chances, cause—'cause of my reputation.

ELAIN. I don't know what you mean—you're perfectly sweet.

CARNELLE. Well, everyone knew I used to go out with lots of men and all that. Different ones. It's been a constant thing with me since I was young and—

ELAIN. Let's not discuss it in all a this heat.

CARNELLE. I just mention it cause it's different now, since Aunt Ronelle died and since—I got that disease.

ELAIN. Please, Carnelle, nobody's profiting by this information!

CARNELLE. Anyway, I go to church now and I'm signed up to where I take an orphan home to dinner once a week or to a movie; and—and I work on the cancer drive here just like you do in Natchez.

ELAIN. That's all very admirable, I'm sure.

CARNELLE. My life has meaning. People aren't calling me, Miss Hot Tamale anymore like they used to. Everything's changed. And being in that contest — it would be such an honor to me . . . I can't explain the half of it.

ELAIN. Well, if you don't make it to the finals, just try to remember that Mama was at her most noblest when she was least attractive.

CARNELLE. I wish you had about a drop a faith in me. I'm not all that ugly.

ELAIN. And I wish you would stop fishing for compliments — 'cause I'm sick and worn out with giving people compliments about themselves!

CARNELLE. (*Overlapping.*) I'm sorry. I'm so, so sorry, I make such stupid blunders. I know you don't think I'm ugly.

ELAIN. (*Overlapping.*) I'm not myself — I'm just not myself. (*She begins brushing her hair. The phone rings. Elain freezes. Carnelle goes to answer it.*) If it's for me — say — say, I'm resting.

CARNELLE. Hello. . . . Oh, hello, Franklin. . . . Yes, she's here. . . . Well, I think she decided not to stop by there. . . . No, she's asleep now. She's gone on to sleep. . . . Well, wait just a minute, I'll go see. (*She puts her hand over the phone.*) He wants me to go wake you up.

ELAIN. (*In a whisper.*) He what! Oh, how inconsiderate can he be! Why, I've been driving all day long in this blazing heat and he doesn't even care if I get my rest. You tell him I'm out dead with exhaustion and you absolutely can not wake me.

CARNELLE. (*She waits a few beats and then says breathlessly into the phone.*) Franklin . . . I absolutely can not wake her. She's out dead with exhaustion. . . . Alright, I'll tell her. Bye, bye. (*She hangs up the phone.*) He says for you to please call him when you wake up.

ELAIN. Oh, he does, does he? Well, he can just sit and wait, cause I'm not calling him — not ever.

CARNELLE. Why not?

ELAIN. Listen Carnation, I think you should know something — I'm not just here on a visit.

CARNELLE. You're not?

ELAIN. No. (*Then after a moment.*) I've left Franklin.

CARNELLE. What?!

ELAIN. Now, remember, it's a sworn secret and not a living soul is to find it out.

19

CARNELLE. I won't say a word to anyone. I swear.

ELAIN. You see, I haven't told Franklin yet and he actually still believes everything is — bearable between us.

CARNELLE. I just can't believe all this. You were so in love. It seemed like Franklin loved you so much. I thought I wanted a man to love me that much.

ELAIN. Yes; he did love me. But it just caused him to follow me around asking, "Do you love me? How much do you love me? Tell me how you love me," till I could shake him till he rattled.

CARNELLE. Then you don't love him anymore?

ELAIN. (*Taking off her jewelry.*) No. He makes me ill.

CARNELLE. How awful.

ELAIN. Yes.

CARNELLE. But what about your two little boys. They need a mother.

ELAIN. Oh, children manage in this world. Don't ask me about them.

CARNELLE. Gosh, Aunt Ronelle said you had it all up there in Natchez; everything — just like a queen in a castle.

ELAIN. I know. I did. I only hope I can stand to give it all up. (*Deeply moved.*) We had such beautiful clocks. I must have a bath. (*She rises.*)

CARNELLE. Elain. (*Elain stops.*) What was it like — when you had it all?

ELAIN. Ah, Carnation! The abundance of treasures merely serves to underline the desperate futility of life. (*She exits upstairs to the bedrooms.*)

CARNELLE. Oh — Tell me more — Please! Tell me more! (*She picks up all of the bags and follows Elain out of the room. The stage is empty for a few moments. Suddenly, the front door opens, Delmount Williams enters. Delmount, 28, is tall and thin with piercing blue eyes and a sallow complexion. He wears a white shirt and a pair of worn out pants. He carries a brown paper bag containing all of his belongings. Leaving the front door ajar, Delmount enters the room. He finds something about the atmosphere loathsome. He sits down and lights up a pipe. He sits smoking for a few moments, taking in the room. Popeye peeps in the front door.*)

POPEYE. (*As she enters.*) Carnelle? Carnelle — (*Spotting Delmount.*) Oh!

20

DELMOUNT. Hello.

POPEYE. Hi. Are you—You're—

DELMOUNT. Delmount Williams. I'm Carnelle's cousin.

POPEYE. Yeah.

DELMOUNT. Well, I don't know where Carnelle is right now.

POPEYE. Oh.

DELMOUNT. You're a friend of hers, I suppose?

POPEYE. Yes. I just met her recently. I'm Popeye Jackson.

DELMOUNT. Popeye? That's an unusual name.

POPEYE. Oh, well. . . . It's not my original name. I wasn't born with it. (*Embarrassed she begins to run on.*) See, what happened was my brother Lucky, he threw a handful a gravel in my eyes and they started stinging and then he give me this brown bottle a drops t'put inside my eyes and telling me it's eye drops but, in fact, it's drops for the ears and then this burning sensation come into my eyes, causing me t'scream out and cry like the devil and after that I got me a pair a glasses and my eyes was bulged out a bit; so folks was calling me, Popeye and the name just stuck with me—Popeye. That's how I got the name.

DELMOUNT. (*After a moment.*) Well, that's a mighty tragic tale.

POPEYE. Ah, no. Actually, the fortunate part is I can now hear voices through my eyes.

DELMOUNT. Through your eyes.

POPEYE. Well, now and then I hear em—laughing and—carrying on.

DELMOUNT. Yeah. Well, I think I'll see if I can rustle up Carnelle for you. Carnelle! Honey! Are you home?! Carnelle! Carnelle!

POPEYE. Oh, no! No! I just forgot these measurements and I see em right here on the side table! (*Carnelle enters from the bedrooms.*)

CARNELLE. Delmount! No! No, it isn't you! Why, I can't believe my eyes! Oh, Popeye, this is my cousin, Delmount! He's come back at last! How are you? Are you doing alright? You look tired.

DELMOUNT. I'm fine. Is that a wig?

CARNELLE. What? Oh, no; it's real.

DELMOUNT. My, God, Child, are you trying to look like a bareback rider in the Shooley Traveling Carnival Show?

CARNELLE. You don't like it?

DELMOUNT. Hardly, Honey. Hardly.

CARNELLE. Maybe you'll grow accustomed to it. I have more and more myself. First I didn't like it at all—thought it was loud, in fact. Ah, did you meet my friend, Popeye?

DELMOUNT. (*Sitting down to smoke his pipe.*) We've spoken. (*Carnelle looks over to Popeye. Popeye manages to smile but stands frozen.*)

CARNELLE. (*Turning back to Delmount.*) Why, look at you! When did you start smoking a pipe?

DELMOUNT. Don't be silly. I've *always* smoked a pipe. Good Lord and butter. (*After a moment to the women.*) Why don't you sit down?

POPEYE. (*Making her exit in a flurry.*) No. I—really have to be going. I just forgot these measurements here. Now I got em.

CARNELLE. Well, alright. I'll be seeing you. Bye! (*Popeye is gone. Carnelle turns back to Delmount.*) So, what have you been doing?

DELMOUNT. Not much. Had a job scraping up dead dogs from the road.

CARNELLE. We were—concerned about you.

DELMOUNT. I was alright. Course the dogs were a rotting mess.

CARNELLE. (*After a moment.*) So, what brings you back home to Brookhaven?

DELMOUNT. Business.

CARNELLE. Oh.

DELMOUNT. I don't know if you realized this but my mamma the monkey left the whole of this house to me.

CARNELLE. I realized it.

DELMOUNT. Well, I'm going to sell it. I'm going to sell this house and every stick of furniture in it. And I don't want to hear anything from you about it. It's mine; it's been given to me. And I'm not going to feel sorry for you just cause you went and dyed your hair fire engine red!

CARNELLE. Well, alright, Delmount! You don't have to get mean about it! If you want to sell the house, it's your house to sell; so go on and sell it!

DELMOUNT. I will! I'm through working at disgusting job

A change of clothes for Elained

after disgusting job. I hate working! I loathe it! (*Elain appears on the staircase in a flowing robe.*)

ELAIN. Carnation, Honey, where'd you put the—

DELMOUNT. Oh—No!!

ELAIN. Delmount!

DELMOUNT. You bitch! You!

ELAIN. What!?

DELMOUNT. How could you betray me like that!?! Your own flesh! Your own blood!

ELAIN. What's wrong with you? Are you still insane?

DELMOUNT. Ooh! Ooh! I'm not speaking to you! I'm not speaking to you!!

CARNELLE. (*Overlapping.*) What's going on? What is it?

ELAIN. Don't ask me! Don't ask me!

DELMOUNT. No! No! Don't ask her! She could never tell. She could never tell that the beautiful, the sweet, the perfect, Elain Rutledge refused to help her own brother get out of a dirty lunatic asylum!

ELAIN. Why, it was clean, it was cheerful, it was the most expensive money could buy! Oh, but you've always lied—even as a child we could never believe a word you said!

CARNELLE. (*Overlapping.*) Oh, what's wrong? What happened? Tell me! Please!!

DELMOUNT. It's all quite simple, Child a Mine. They would have released me after two months time into Mrs. Rutledge's loving custody, cause, you see, she is my next a kin, but she wouldn't have me. She wouldn't sign the papers.

ELAIN. (*Overlapping.*) Please, Delmount. I'm sorry, but we thought you needed the professional help. You were so upset about Mama dying—

DELMOUNT. Oh, Lord! She knows I wasn't upset cause of that! She know's that!

ELAIN. And Franklin just thought, cause of the children—

DELMOUNT. (*Under his breath.*) Franklin—that sheep pussy.

ELAIN. (*Angry.*) I mean, after all, Delmount, you did commit a violent act—hitting that poor man in the face with a bottle—

DELMOUNT. (*To Carnelle.*) Do you actually think I'm of such base character? I challenged that man to a duel! A duel! I can't help it if the weapons he chose were broken bottles! It was an

23

honorable act in defense of a woman with beautiful, warm, bronze skin. I do not regret it.

ELAIN. (*Trying to break in between Carnelle and Delmount.*) Well, besides all of that, you know good and well, you've always had a checkered past!

DELMOUNT. What checkered past?

ELAIN. For one thing, you tried to choke Carnelle's poor father to death right in there at the dining room table!

DELMOUNT. Why, I never!

ELAIN. You did! It was right on New Year's Day!

CARNELLE. That's right, cause I found the dime in the black-eyed peas —

DELMOUNT. Alright, I did! I did it! But he was boring me to death! I just wanted to shut him up!

ELAIN. Now, see! See! That is not reasonable behavior! It's just not reasonable. And how you almost got run out of town on a rail cause of what happened with T.S. Mahoney's two young virgin daughters! It's no wonder you have bad dreams! It's no wonder!!

DELMOUNT. Rub my face in it, why don't you! You're so damn perfect and I'm such a no account failure! Rub my face in it!

ELAIN. I'm sorry Delmount. I'm sorry. Oh, you bring out the worst in me. You always have. You always have! (*Elain exits in a flurry. Carnelle and Delmount look after her for a moment then Carnelle goes to pick up the crackers and Delmount goes back to his pipe.*)

DELMOUNT. The irony of it. The intense irony.

CARNELLE. What irony?

DELMOUNT. Mahoney's two ugly daughters. I went up there thinking all they wanted was for me to see their box of newborn kittens. Well, when we got up in the attic, I saw most all of the kittens had swollen heads and crippled bodies. It was nothing but a cardboard box full of deformed damn cats. That's all there was to it. Well, I felt sorry for those two ugly daughters with their deformed box of cats. And they were dying for it. Hell, I was doing them a favor. There's the irony. You just can't go around obliging other people in this world. That's one thing I've learned.

CARNELLE. (*Sticking a dirty cracker into her mouth.*) I feel sorry for ugly girls. I really do.

24

DELMOUNT. Yeah. Ah, listen, little Child a Mine. About selling the house and all, I was planning on giving you half of what I make. That way you can get out of this town for good and always. How about it?

CARNELLE. Well, Delmount. I don't know! I've never thought about leaving Brookhaven.

DELMOUNT. Well, think about it. There's never been anything here for you but sorrow.

CARNELLE. Yes, that's true. Still . . . I don't know. (*After a moment.*) Maybe if I could, if I could leave in a blaze of glory! Yes! That's what I'd like to do — leave this town in a blaze of glory!

DELMOUNT. How do you mean?

CARNELLE. Well, if I won the Miss Firecracker Contest — See, I'm a contestant in it and if I could just win first prize then I would be able to leave this town in a crimson blaze of glory!

DELMOUNT. The Miss Firecracker Contest — Hell and damnation! (*He gets up.*)

CARNELLE. (*Following after him.*) Where are you going?

DELMOUNT. For a walk! (*He exits out the front door.*)

CARNELLE. (*Yelling after him.*) Delmount! Well, what in the world is eating you?! (*After a moment.*) Hmm, yes . . . a crimson blaze of glory! (*She performs with solemn beauty as the lights begin to fade.*) "And the rockets red glare — Boom! — the bombs bursting in air — Boom! — gave proof through the night — that our flag was — Boom! — there!" Boom! Boom! Boom!

BLACKOUT

END OF SCENE

ACT I

Scene Two

The lights go up on the living room. It is about eight o'clock in the evening on the following Saturday. Several cold, formal arrangements of long stemmed roses have been placed around the room. Most pieces of furniture now have price tags tied onto

evening dolly

*them. Delmount stands smoking a pipe, and spinning the spin-
ning wheel around as he listens to it creak.*

DELMOUNT. Hmmm. . . . (*He gives the spinning wheel a kick.
It wobbles. He goes to the desk to fill out a price tag. Elain enters carrying
a silver tray with a decanter of wine and three glasses on it. One of the
glasses has already been poured. Elain is somewhat tipsy.*)

ELAIN. Hello, Delly, I've brought you out a cool glass of Japanese plum wine.

DELMOUNT. No, thank you.

ELAIN. (*Setting the tray down.*) It's really exquisite wine. I just
love things that are Japanese. (*He doesn't respond.*) Sure you don't
want a glass?

DELMOUNT. Yes. (*He goes to put a price tag on the spinning
wheel.*)

ELAIN. How much are you asking for the spinning wheel?

DELMOUNT. Five dollars.

ELAIN. Five dollars! Why, that is just wildly ridiculous! I
mean, that's an actual antique you've got before you!

DELMOUNT. If you don't mind, Miss Priss, this is all my af-
fair!

ELAIN. Ooh. And I thought you weren't mad at me anymore.

DELMOUNT. What made you think that?

ELAIN. Yesterday afternoon when we were sitting out back
snapping green beans for supper you started laughing and telling your stories—I thought we were friends again. Please, you
know you're just being hard-hearted about the whole thing.

DELMOUNT. I don't know what I'm being. I had bad dreams
last night. I always have them. They never stop. Every night I
have them.

ELAIN. (*Fanning herself.*) Must a been the heat. (*The phone
rings. They look at each other.*) Get it!! (*Delmount dashes for the phone.
Carnelle appears at the door with a dish rag in her hand. It is obvious that
she has raced to get there.*)

DELMOUNT. (*Answering the phone.*) Hello? . . . This is he
speaking . . . Yes . . . What? . . . No, I would not consider
giving it away . . . I'm sorry but I happen to need the profit
. . . (*Carnelle goes and picks up Delmount's dinner tray that is sitting on
the desk.*) Well, it'll be up for auction at the July Fourth Carnival, if you want it so badly you can bid for it there . . . Yes

26

— apron evening clothing

. . . Fine. Good-bye. (*He hangs up the phone.*) That was Mrs.
J.R. Biggs. Imagine! She wanted me to donate that old spinning wheel to the D.A.R. How ludicrous! As though that entire
organization couldn't afford to bid five dollars for it! What
presumption! It's most maddening!

CARNELLE. Well, I guess, I better go and finish up the
dishes. That—ah, that tuna nood'll really stick t'your plates.
(*She exits to the kitchen, holding back tears.*)

DELMOUNT. Dammit! When were they supposed to have
called by?

ELAIN. Six o'clock. It's after eight now.

DELMOUNT. I hate this. So she didn't even make it to the
stupid finals.

ELAIN. I guess not.

DELMOUNT. God.

ELAIN. Not only that—Ruby Kay told me this year they had
the worst turn out in history. Ever since they had to integrate
the contest she says the turn out's been decreasing and the quality of the entire event has gone down, down, down.

DELMOUNT. Oh, stop it, please! I don't want to hear about
it. Jesus God.

ELAIN. I know, I know.

DELMOUNT. (*Frantically.*) I don't know what to do. I mean,
she actually thinks she's tap dancing. (*He imitates her.*) She's
moving around like this, or something and she thinks she's tap
dancing. Remember how Uncle Willie just dropped her off here
and left her with nothing but a pillow case full of dirty rags? I'd
never seen anything so pathetic. Had ringworms in her head.

ELAIN. Uh. Mama had to shave off all of her hair and put
ointment on those sores in her head—I don't know, seemed like
several times a day.

DELMOUNT. God, she was an ugly sight.

ELAIN. Wasn't she though. She always went around wearing
that yellow wool knit cap pulled down over her head even in the
summer's heat. Mama told her people would just think she had
short yellow hair.

DELMOUNT. Mama was such a brilliant woman.

ELAIN. Well, from a distance it kinda looked like that.

DELMOUNT. I do doubt it. Anyway, she never did attain any
self-esteem. Had to sleep with every worthless soul in Brookhaven trying to prove she was attractive.

27

ELAIN. (*Finishing another glass of wine.*) Please! It was just some sort of degrading stage she was going through. I'm certain she's over it now.

DELMOUNT. Well, I wish she was back in it.

ELAIN. Delmount!

DELMOUNT. I do! Least then she wasn't putting herself into stupid, miserable contests and publicly getting kicked in the face. Least for the disease she just privately took some shots.

ELAIN. Don't talk about it! I can't bear that side of life! It's repulsive to me. So shut up your mouth for once!!

DELMOUNT. Well, don't have a hissy fit! (*The phone rings.*)

ELAIN. My, God.

DELMOUNT. You think it's them?

ELAIN. No. I don't know. (*Carnelle appears at the door with a brownie in her hand.*)

CARNELLE. Here, I'll get it. I'll go on and—get it. (*She picks up the phone.*) Hello? . . . Oh. Yes, just a minute. It's for you Elain. It's Franklin.

ELAIN. Thanks. (*Carnelle exits to the kitchen, stuffing the brownie into her mouth.*) Hello. . . . Yes, Dear, I got them. . . . Oh, they're beautiful; they're—very fragrant; they're—I-I don't want to come home. . . . I mean not ever, or for awhile, or for not ever. . . . I feel like I'm missing my life. . . . I don't know about the children. They'll manage. . . . Oh, for God's sake, Franklin, no one's going to bake them into a pie! . . . Oh, please! I don't want to discuss it anymore. I'm tired of it all, I'm through with it all. Good-bye! (*She hangs up the phone. She is stunned and shaken by what she has done.*)

DELMOUNT. (*Who has been listening to all of this while pretending to work with the price tags.*) Did you mean it? You're gonna leave him?

ELAIN. Yes.

DELMOUNT. By God, Swayne. By God. I love ya, Honey! How I do love ya! Now are you sure you meant it?

ELAIN. Uh huh.

DELMOUNT. Don't just tell me you meant it, then later take it all back. You've done that before, you know.

ELAIN. I haven't.

DELMOUNT. What do you mean you haven't?!? It's a personality trait with you. It's your trademark! You tell me you're gonna do something one way and then you go back on it cause of what Mama said or what Franklin said or what some other fly-by-night-fool-idiot said!

ELAIN. Don't pick on me!

DELMOUNT. Ooh! I knew it! You didn't mean it! I knew it!

ELAIN. I meant it! I said it!

DELMOUNT. All you want is for everyone to think you're perfect. Well, perfect is dull!

ELAIN. Don't you dare call me dull. Just because I'm not insane and obsessed and possessed by dreams.

DELMOUNT. (*Overlapping.*) Shut up, Elain. Shut up your red blood lips!

ELAIN. You are a selfish human being! Mama always loved you ten times better than me.

DELMOUNT. Oh God.

ELAIN. I had to win contests and be in pageants before she'd give me any notice at all. When I graduated Jr. college she said, "You've had your spoonful of gravy now go out and get a rich husband;" so I did.

DELMOUNT. You're a fool to let Mama ramshackle your life. Mama was nothing but mean.

ELAIN. Not to you. She was sweet to you.

DELMOUNT. She pretended to be sweet.

ELAIN. Well, everyone always thought she was. Till the day she died, people were saying she was a blessed angel on earth.

DELMOUNT. Yeah, an angel in apes clothing.

ELAIN. You are so cruel.

DELMOUNT. Well, hell, she just turned herself into a monkey to get at us—just to be mean. I always knew Mama was mean.

ELAIN. No. She wasn't always. Things change. She wasn't always.

DELMOUNT. Why, I remember when I was a child a three how she tortured our favorite dog, White Face, right before my very eyes.

ELAIN. Wha'd she do to White Face?

DELMOUNT. Well, remember how White Face would always stand out by the back porch door hoping somebody would throw him some measly scraps?

ELAIN. I guess so.

29

DELMOUNT. Well, one day she was making a lemon pie and she says to me, "Ha! Let's see how he likes *this!*" and she slings a lemon rind right out to White Face and he jumps up and bites into it then runs off howling. And she's just standing there — laughing.

ELAIN. (*Stunned.*) Oh my God. So, Mama's always been mean. G'me a drag off a your pipe. (*He hands her the pipe. She takes a long drag.*)

DELMOUNT. Are you really gonna leave him?

ELAIN. (*Handing back the pipe.*) I said I would. (*The phone rings. They look at each other.*)

DELMOUNT. I can't stand it. (*He grabs the phone angrily.*) Yeah!? . . . Oh. Yes, just a minute. Carnelle? Carnelle, telephone!! Carnelle!

ELAIN. (*Overlapping.*) Carnelle! Honey! Phone! (*Carnelle appears. Her face is beet red.*)

CARNELLE. For me?

DELMOUNT. Uh huh. (*He hands her the phone.*)

CARNELLE. (*Into the phone.*) Hello. . . . Oh, Ronnie. . . . No, I don't think so. . . . Cause, I don't go out riding around like that anymore. I got other interests now. . . . You just don't understand anything about me. . . . Now don't you call me that. . . . I said don't call me that. So long. (*She hangs up the phone and stands totally still.*)

ELAIN. Who was it?

CARNELLE. Nobody. Just that creep Ronnie Wayne I used to date. He's calling me Miss Hot Tamale. Listen, I guess, I won't be needing that red dress of yours. It looks like I didn't make the Miss Firecracker Contest after all.

DELMOUNT. Ah well . . . count yourself lucky — that type a false pageantry; it's way beneath you.

ELAIN. Yes, it is. Why-why since it's been integrated the quality of the contest has really gone down, down, down.

DELMOUNT. Why, it's nothing but a garish display of painted up prancing pigs! That's all there is to it.

CARNELLE. Well, the main thing is — it was gonna be — I don't know — visible proof. And I would a liked to ride on a float and wave out to people.

ELAIN. Why, all this is gonna help build up your character! Remember, the more Mama suffered the more divine she became. (*There is a knock at the door.*)

CARNELLE. That must be Popeye. I told her I'd pay her to-night for sewing my costume. Tell her I'll be right back with the money. (*She exits up the stairs, holding back tears.*)

DELMOUNT. Popeye—that's all we need. Did she lose her brains or what?

ELAIN. I like Popeye. She's a nice girl.

DELMOUNT. Then you talk to her. I'm gonna go get my dessert. (*He exits to the kitchen, mumbling to himself.*) So, it's over. It's finished. She lost. Good. I'm glad!

ELAIN. (*As she opens the door for Popeye.*) Hello, Honey. Come on in. (*Popeye enters. She is wearing the earrings.*) ~~—————————~~ *a old evening dress homemade*,

POPEYE. Hi.

ELAIN. Well, it looks like our little Carnation didn't make the beauty pageant after all.

POPEYE. (*Shocked.*) She didn't?

ELAIN. No.

POPEYE. I can't believe it.

ELAIN. Well, here, Honey, let me get you a glass of cool, plum wine.

POPEYE. I just knew she was gonna make it—with her red hair and her dancing and those roman candles shooting off right up into the sky.

ELAIN. (*Handing her some wine.*) I know. She put a lot of work into it. It's a disappointment. But life is hard and it's never easy to lose anything.

POPEYE. No, I suppose not. (*After a moment.*) I once knew these two midgets by the names of Sweet Pea and Willas. I went to their wedding and they was the only midgets there. Rest a their family was regular size people. But they was so happy together and they moved into a little midget house where everything was mite size like this little old desk they had and this little ole stool. Then Sweet Pea got pregnant and later on she had what they called this Caesarean birth where they slice open your stomach and pull the baby out from the slice. Well, come to find out, the babies a regular size child and soon that baby is just too large for Sweet Pea to carry around and too large for all a that mite sized furniture. So Sweet Pea has to give up her own baby for her Mama to raise. I thought she'd die to lose that child. It about crushed her heart.

31

ELAIN. (*Finishing off her glass of wine.*) I don't feel that way about my two boys. I don't want to spend time teaching them manners. I don't like them.

POPEYE. Y'don't?

ELAIN. No. My husband either.

POPEYE. What's wrong with him?

ELAIN. (*Gayly, as she pours herself some more wine.*) He smells of sweet cologne and wears three rings on every finger.

POPEYE. (*Pretending she has three rings on every finger.*) Gosh. They must feel heavy.

ELAIN. It's such a burden trying to live up to a beautiful face. I'm afraid I'm missing everything in the world. (*Delmount enters from the kitchen.*)

DELMOUNT. What happened to all of those brownies?

ELAIN. They're right in there on that blue china tray.

DELMOUNT. All of them?

ELAIN. Yes, Delly, the whole batch. (*Delmount exits to the kitchen.*)

POPEYE. (*Whispering hoarsely.*) What's the matter? He can't find the brownies?

ELAIN. I'm sure they're right under his nose. (*Delmount enters, carrying an empty tray.*)

DELMOUNT. They're all gone! The whole batch!

ELAIN. My, goodness! Well, I guess Carnelle ate them up. She's a compulsive eater when she's unhappy.

DELMOUNT. Dammit! I wanted a brownie! (*Then he stops, embarrassed.*) Ah, hello, Popeye. How're you?

POPEYE. Fine.

DELMOUNT. (*Smoothing down his wild hair.*) Well. . . . good. Ah, lovely earrings you're wearing.

POPEYE. Thank you. They was a present t'me from Elain. She give em to me.

DELMOUNT. Oh, right. Carnelle mentioned it . . . Well, maybe we—have some ice cream in the freezer. (*He exits to the kitchen.*)

POPEYE. (*Weakly.*) Oh. Oh. Oh. (*She begins fanning her heart and blowing air onto it.*)

ELAIN. What's the matter? Are you alright?

POPEYE. My heart—it's—hot. It's hot. It's burning. (*Blowing air onto her heart.*) Puff, puff, puff. (*She puts the wine glass against her heart.*) There. Ah. It's better now. It's better.

ELAIN. My word, you look faint.

POPEYE. Tell me, when your heart gets hot, does that mean you're in love?

ELAIN. Dar'lin, are you in love?

POPEYE. I reckon.

ELAIN. Not — not with Delmount?!

POPEYE. Yes. (*Puff, puff.*) Yes.

ELAIN. How astonishing! Why, his complexion's so sallow — and he's got a rude, irritable disposition.

POPEYE. It does seem like it.

ELAIN. How utterly odd. Tell me, Popeye, have you ever been in love before?

POPEYE. Well, my heart's never been hot or nothing, but I did have me a boyfriend once.

ELAIN. And what was he like?

POPEYE. Not much. He like t'pet me like I was a cat or something. He's asking me to purr and meow. Like, "meow, meow, purr, purr, purr." I don't know, he's crazy. I's expecting him t'give me a box a cat nips for Christmas.

ELAIN. What did he give you?

POPEYE. . . . Nothing.

ELAIN. (*Pouring them both more wine.*) Well, if you want my opinion, that is just about what Delmount will give you. He's an unstable character and he's had a very checkered past.

POPEYE. I know bout that.

ELAIN. Well, did you know about his strange, obsessive eye for beauty? (*Popeye shakes her head.*) How he's been known to follow a normal looking woman through the streets all day and all night because he finds the mere shape of her nose exotic or beautiful; or perhaps he finds the texture of her lips to be unusually soft and smooth. You don't want anything to do with him. I worry about him. He's not right. He's obsessed. (*She finishes her drink. She is uncomfortable and upset.*) What in the world is keeping Carnelle? She must be up in her room crying. I'd better go get her. (*Elain exits up the stairs. Popeye sits alone sipping wine. She begins shaking her head back and forth. After a momer; she makes a solemn toast to the voices inside her eyes.*)

POPEYE. Cheers. (*Delmount enters from the kitchen. He is eating a dish of vanilla ice cream.*)

DELMOUNT. Oh. Hello. Where's Elain?

POPEYE. She's getting Carnelle.

DELMOUNT. (*Smoothing down his hair.*) Oh. (*He sits at the desk and begins writing.*)

POPEYE. Are you writing poems?

DELMOUNT. What?

POPEYE. Carnelle said you write poems.

DELMOUNT. Oh. Well, on occasion I have.

POPEYE. I'd like to read em.

DELMOUNT. (*Embarrassed.*) They're personal.

POPEYE. Oh. (*She starts to run on.*) Course, I never read many poems before. There weren't all that many poem books you could get off a the traveling book mobil. Most books I got was about animals. Farm animals, jungle animals, arctic animals and such. Course they was informative, I learned some things; they's called: a gaggle a geese; a pride a lions; a warren a rabbits; a host a whales. That's my personal favorite one: a host a whales! (*They look at each other.*) Carnelle says you can wiggle your ears.

DELMOUNT. Does she?

POPEYE. Yes.

DELMOUNT. (*Straightening his hair.*) It's an old trick.

POPEYE. I would liked t'have seen it.

DELMOUNT. I don't do it anymore. (*He straightens his hair again.*)

POPEYE. What d'ya dream about at nights?

DELMOUNT. (*Taken aback.*) Why do you ask?

POPEYE. I don't know, you're face looks tired. I thought maybe you was having bad dreams.

DELMOUNT. What are you saying? You make me uncomfortable. A gaggle of geese! What's that?! What are you talking about? This whole night has been unbearable! Ooooh! Now the ice cream has given me a headache. Lord Jesus! A gaggle of geese! Oh, my head! My, head! (*He exits to the bedroom, holding his head. Popeye watches him leave then she puts both of her hands over her heart and starts to sob.*)

POPEYE. Oh. Oh. Oh. I must be stupid. I must be. (*CAR-*

NELLE enters from the bedrooms. Her nose is red. She carries a wad of kleenexes and a change purse. She spots Popeye crying.)

CARNELLE. Popeye! What is it? What's the matter?

POPEYE. (*Sobbing.*) Oh, I'm stupid. I'm stupid.

CARNELLE. Why? What happened? What?

POPEYE. It seems — It seems I love him. (*Pointing to the door.*) I love Delmount.

CARNELLE. Oh, no! I knew it. I knew it.

POPEYE. But I don't know what to say. I don't know how to come to say it. I just say, "Carnelle says you can wiggle your ears." He doesn't love me. I've lost him!

CARNELLE. (*Starting to cry.*) Oh, oh. Dear, little Popeye. I've lost too. I've lost too.

POPEYE. What?

CARNELLE. The contest! I lost the Miss Firecracker Contest!

POPEYE. Oh, right.

CARNELLE. I didn't even make the finals! They don't want me. I'm a failure!

POPEYE. Oh! There, there.

CARNELLE. I'm ugly, Popeye! My thighs are fat! No one loves me!

POPEYE. (*Overlapping.*) Oh, he'll never love me! Never! Never!! Oh, I hope I don't scream out — aaahh!!!

CARNELLE. (*Overlapping as she pulls at her hair.*) I hate my hair! I hate it! (*Elain enters from the bedroom. She spots them crying.*)

ELAIN. My, God! What is it? What's wrong?! Did someone die?!

CARNELLE. (*Falling across the couch.*) Oh, don't ask! Don't ask!

ELAIN. What happened?! Please! What?!

POPEYE. (*Wiping away tears.*) Well . . . well, she's crying cause she lost the beauty contest — and, and I'm crying cause he — he — he doesn't care about me! (*Popeye breaks down crying.*)

ELAIN. Oh, I see. You poor dears. You poor dears. There, there now. Here, here, now. There, there. (*Popeye and Carnelle whimper softly.*) You don't have to worry anymore. Things'll get better. Your lives aren't over, not like mine is. No neither of you have to face the sort of tragedy I'm facing. Neither of you is starting life all over again, feeling nothing but terror and fear and loneliness! (*Popeye and Carnelle sob loudly.*) Oh, God. Oh,

God. I can't believe I've left him. I've left him! Oh, my, dear God! There'll be no more roses! No more! (*She caresses an armful of roses.*)

CARNELLE. What? You've really left Franklin?

ELAIN. Yes! (*Weeping as she throws a handful of roses.*) Good-bye!

CARNELLE. You've told him?

ELAIN. (*Throwing another handful of roses.*) Yes! Farewell!

CARNELLE. Oh, Elain! Elain!

ELAIN. (*Throwing roses.*) No, more! No, more!!

POPEYE. Roses! Look! Roses!

ELAIN. (*Throwing roses.*) I don't know what to do! I don't know what I can do!

CARNELLE. Me neither; me neither. Oh, life!

POPEYE. (*Holding roses.*) Roses! Roses! Roses! (*Pause. The phone rings. All throw roses at the phone as they continue weeping.*)

POPEYE. (*Pointing to the phone with a rose.*) It rings!

ELAIN. Oh, let it ring! Just let it ring!

POPEYE. Yes, ring! (*The phone rings four more times.*)

CARNELLE. (*Suddenly alive.*) Wait. I'll get it. Quick! Here, I'll get it! (*She grabs the receiver.*) Hello. . . . Yes, this is she. . . . What? . . . Oh, I'm so sorry. . . . Oh, no. How sad. How tragic. . . . What? . . . Yes, alright. . . . Thank you. Bye bye. (*She puts down the phone.*) That—That was Miss Blue and, well, do you remember her little dog, Turnip?

ELAIN. The brown and white one—

CARNELLE. (*Breathlessly.*) Yes, well, Turnip was hit by a van and he died; so Miss Blue was late in notifying the five finalists but—oh my God.

POPEYE. Huh?

CARNELLE. Oh my God.

ELAIN. What?

CARNELLE. I made. I made it! By God I made the pageant!!! I did! I did! I made it! AAAHHH!!!!!

ELAIN. (*Overlapping.*) Praise God! Praise God! Some victory!

POPEYE. (*Overlapping.*) Oh you made it! You made it! Hurray!

ELAIN. (*Running on.*) Oh, Carnation! Carnation, what a triumph for you! Of course, I always knew you'd make the pageant! I never doubted it for one minute!

CARNELLE. They're—they're gonna be taking my picture for

the newspaper at ten o'clock in the morning at the Court House square. I'll be famous!

ELAIN. It's just stupendous! Here; here let's have a toast!

CARNELLE. A toast for *me?* Make a toast for *me?*

ELAIN. Yes! Yes! (*She starts to pour the glasses.*)

POPEYE. Yes, a toast! A toast!

ELAIN. Quick, call Delmount! I'll pour out these glasses.

CARNELLE. Delmount! Delmount, come quick! We're having a toast! We're having a toast to me!

ELAIN. (*Overlapping.*) Here, you go, Popeye. And for our Carnation. (*Delmount enters from the bathroom. He is in his bathrobe and wears a towel wrapped around his head.*)

DELMOUNT. What is it? What? I'm right in the middle of my hot oil treatment!

ELAIN. (*Handing him a glass.*) Here, Delmount, we're having a toast!

DELMOUNT. Huh?

ELAIN. Well, no more glasses. I'll just have to drink from the bottle. A toast everyone! To Carnation! May she win first prize in the Miss Firecracker Contest!

DELMOUNT. What?!

ELAIN. (*She raises the bottle.*) Cheers!

POPEYE. (*Raising her glass.*) Cheers!

CARNELLE. (*Raising her glass.*) Cheers!

DELMOUNT. (*As he clicks each of their glasses.*) Oh — my — miserable — God! (*They go about clicking each other's glasses as Delmount downs his drink and the lights blackout.*)

END OF ACT I

SYNOPSIS OF SCENES

SCENE ONE: The carnival grounds—about three o'clock in the afternoon on the Fourth of July.

We see the outside area behind a large carnival tent and the inside of a backstage dressing room. There is simply a bench and a garbage can in the outside area. To get to this area the characters enter from right. It should be established that when entering from down right the characters are coming from a different part of the carnival then when entering from up right.

The characters can get to the dressing room from this outside area by taking a step up and entering through a doorway. Inside the dressing room there is a dressing table, a chair, a stool, and a clothes rack. There is a curtain in the dressing room at left. This entrance and exit leads to the backstage area of the beauty contest.

SCENE TWO: The same setting. Several minutes later.

SCENE THREE: The same setting. That evening.

ACT II

Scene One

The lights go up on an empty stage. Mac Sam, the balloon man enters up right carrying a bunch of colored balloons, and coughing painfully. Mac Sam is in his mid-thirties. He is amazingly· thin; stooped shouldered; and in drastically poor health. Yet there is something extraordinarily sensual about him. His eyes manage to be magnetic and bloodshot at the same time. He walks slowly over to the doorway of the dressing room.

MAC SAM. Hey, Carnelle. Hey, beautiful. (*He sees that no one is inside.*) Hmm. (*He finishes his cigarette and tosses it to the ground and spits up a lot of blood. He wanders off up* R., *coughing and whistling a tune. Carnelle enters* L. *into the dressing room with Tessy Mahoney. Tessy is the uglier of T.S. Mahoney's two ugly daughters. She has a large nose, a weak chin, tiny eyes and bad posture. She covers up her bitterness by being as sweet as she can be. Carnelle is wearing a simple button down shift but she has applied lavish makeup and elaborately styled her hair in preparation for the contest. Both women are carrying armloads of beauty contest paraphernalia: the red antebellum dress; a hoop for the skirt; pantaloons; the red, silver and blue costume; a robe; a make-up case; shoes; stockings; roman candles; etc.*)

TESSY. (*As she enters the dressing room carrying only the tap shoes.*) It's over here. It's this way. It's this way, here!

CARNELLE'S VOICE. Oh. Oh, I see. I see!

TESSY. Can you make it?

CARNELLE. (*Making her way into the dressing room.*) Yeah. I got it. Here, I got it. (*Dropping her belongings where she can.*) Wheew! Brother. Thanks very much for the help.

TESSY. Sure. It's what I'm here for.

CARNELLE. Oh, look! Is this my dressing room? Is this mine?

TESSY. (*Picking up her clipboard and taking a pencil from behind her ear.*) Uh huh. It's the only one left. The good ones have all been taken. (*Looking at her watch.*) You're running late, you know.

CARNELLE. (*Struggling with her belongings.*) Yes, I know. I was sewing on my dress. Things aren't going smoothly at all today.

39

Oh, look! Now my hair piece is falling out. I worked all morning on that. So, is your sister nervous?

TESSY. Not really. I guess she knows she doesn't have a chance.

CARNELLE. (*As she straightens up her things.*) What makes you say that?

TESSY. Well, she's not at all attractive. I'm amazed she ever got in the contest. I'm sure it's just cause the judges think she's some sort of concert pianist. But she just knows that one opus by Johann Sebastian Bach. I swear that's all she knows.

CARNELLE. Hmm, I suppose that talent part of the contest will count quite a bit.

TESSY. Well, she looks like a tank in her swim suit.

CARNELLE. She does?

TESSY. She's hump shouldered from practicing that one Johann Sebastian Bach opus on our piano all day long.

CARNELLE. What a shame.

TESSY. This is strictly confidential, but the word is out that the only real contenders for the Miss Firecracker crown are you and Caroline Jeffers.

CARNELLE. (*Overcome.*) Oh, gosh, I don't know—

TESSY. It's the truth. Everyone's saying it. We're all agreed.

CARNELLE. Of course Caroline's really a lovely girl . . .

TESSY. Yeah, except for those yellow teeth.

CARNELLE. Well, I hear she took medicine for seizures that she had as a child and it scraped off most of her tooth enamel.

TESSY. I heard that too, but it doesn't matter.

CARNELLE. It doesn't?

TESSY. I really don't think the judges are interested in sentimentality—just the teeth themselves. (*Referring to the red dress.*) That's such a beautiful red dress. It's really very fine.

CARNELLE. Yes, it's beautiful. I'm just a little worried though. It just arrived from Natchez yesterday and, well, it didn't seem to fit me exactly right.

TESSY. What's wrong with the fit?

CARNELLE. Well, the waist was a little snug. But I worked on it this morning and added in this extra bit of material. (*She shows that a large strip of pink material has been awkwardly added to the bodice of the red dress.*)

TESSY. (*Disdainfully.*) Oh. Well.

40

CARNELLE. Course, I know it's not the exact matching color. Actually, my cousin, Elain's gone to get my seamstress, Popeye Jackson, and see what she can do. We couldn't find her last night. She'll fix it right up. This is just temporary.

TESSY. Well, I hope so. It looks a little funny.

CARNELLE. (*Looking outside.*) Oh, I know Elain'll bring Popeye; she promised she would. She's never let me down in her life. Gosh, I think I'm starting t'sweat. My makeup is melting right down my face. (*She starts fixing her face.*)

TESSY. (*Looking at her watch.*) Hmm. Actually, you don't have much time. It's only twenty-eight minutes till the opening Parade of Firecrackers. (*Tessy blows her whistle.*)

CARNELLE. Oh, my word! Well, I'm ready except for my dress. I mean, my head is ready.

TESSY. (*Removing schedule from her clipboard.*) Well, anyway, here's your schedule.

CARNELLE. Thanks.

TESSY. Oh and have you seen the Grand Float they've made for Miss Firecracker to ride at the head of the Independence Day Parade?

CARNELLE. Oh, yes, I saw it — it's . . . beautiful.

TESSY. Why, yes, it's very fine. Well, I'd better go let Miss Blue know you're checked in. (*After glancing at herself in the mirror.*) Oh. Mind if I borrow some of your hairspray?

CARNELLE. No, go ahead.

TESSY. Thanks. (*As she sprays her already rock hard hair.*) I, ah, hear your cousin Delmount's back in town.

CARNELLE. Yes, he's back.

TESSY. (*Still spraying.*) Well, you can tell him for me that I've forgiven him. I understand now that some men just don't have any self control. Just none at all. Think that'll hold?

CARNELLE. Uh huh.

TESSY. Anyway, tell him my Uncle Ferd's given us a new litter of siamese kittens if he wants to drop by and see them. I know he always enjoyed animals.

CARNELLE. I'll tell him.

TESSY. Well, good luck. I'll be standing by backstage running the contest. Let me know if any emergencies arrive.

CARNELLE. Alright.

TESSY. Give em H.

CARNELLE. I'll try. (*Tessy exits* L. *Carnelle turns back and looks in the mirror. She stares at herself as she wipes sweat off the back of her neck.*)

CARNELLE. Oh, Lord. (*She tries a big friendly smile. It falters.*) Oh, Lord. (*She begins fooling with her hair and makeup. Mac Sam enters from the carnival grounds* U.R. *He stops; looks at the dressing room; ties his balloons to the bench; and goes toward the dressing room.*)

MAC SAM. (*Looking inside the dressing room.*) Hi, ya!

CARNELLE. AAH!

MAC SAM. Admiring y'physiognomy?

CARNELLE. (*Catching her breath.*) Mac Sam. What are you doing here?

MAC SAM. Just came t'wish you well. Heard you were in the beauty contest and came by t'wish you well.

CARNELLE. (*Breathlessly.*) Thanks. I'm nervous.

MAC SAM. Sure y'are. Well, good luck. I wish y'well. (*He leaves the dressing room. She follows.*)

CARNELLE. I—didn't think I'd be seeing you again.

MAC SAM. Yeah, well, wonders never do quite cease. (*He looks at her with his magnetic eyes then starts to leave again.*)

CARNELLE. I tried to notify you. After I found out. Couldn't . . . locate you though.

MAC SAM. Oh, "that". Yeah, well, I'm enjoying, "that." Find it most fascinating.

CARNELLE. But didn't you get the shots?

MAC SAM. Nah.

CARNELLE. But all you do is—they give you these shots and you're cured. It cures you.

MAC SAM. I don't care t'be cured.

CARNELLE. What do you mean? You've got to be.

MAC SAM. (*Taking out a cigarette.*) Listen, Honey, this life a mine is strictly on the house. Strictly a free roll a the eternal dice. I was almost choked to death by my mama's umbilical cord at birth. Spent three days purple and gasping for breath. I'm tired out of gasping. (*He lights his cigarette and blows out the match.*) Mmm. You're hair looks really nice. I like that color. It looks good on you.

CARNELLE. It doesn't seem too loud?

MAC SAM. (*Smelling her hair.*) Not a bit. No, Sugar, not a bit.

DELMOUNT'S VOICE. Carnelle!? Carnelle, are you about?!

42

CARNELLE. (*Calling.*) Delmount! Is that you? (*To Mac Sam.*) It's my cousin, Delmount.

DELMOUNT'S VOICE. Carnelle!!

CARNELLE. I'm over here!

MAC SAM. Well, I'll be ambling along. It was good seeing you.

CARNELLE. (*Impulsively.*) Will ya come back by?

MAC SAM. (*His eyes becoming magnetic.*) Oh, yeah. (*He exits* R.)

DELMOUNT'S VOICE. Carnelle!

CARNELLE. I'm over here!!! (*Delmount enters excitedly from the carnival grounds* D.R. *His hair is wild; he carries a stuffed dog.*)

DELMOUNT. Oh! Well, there you are! Sounded like your voice was coming from over there by the snow cone stand.

CARNELLE. No, I'm here.

DELMOUNT. Well . . . well, look, here's an artificial dog I won pitching dimes onto plates. Take it; it's for you if you want it.

CARNELLE. Why, thank you, Delmount. (*She kisses him.*) Oh my lips. (*Carnelle hurries into the dressing room to fix her lips. Delmount follows.*)

DELMOUNT. Things are going very good over at the auction. I mean, the furniture, it all seems to be selling like hot cakes. Why, it looks to me, Child a Mine, that our lives may actually be on the verge of being fine.

CARNELLE. Gosh, everything feels so all of a sudden. Selling the house and all of the belongings and . . . leaving. . . . It makes it much more important that I win the contest. I mean, the main thing is I gotta leave in the blaze of glory. (*She leaves the dressing room and starts pacing back and forth.*) Let's see, I know I'll beat Saphire Mendoze just cause she's the token Negro and Mexican. I'm not trying to be mean about it, but it's the truth. Then there's Joe Anne Jacobs.

DELMOUNT. Frank Jacob's sister's in the pageant?

CARNELLE. Uh huh.

DELMOUNT. She's a shrimp.

CARNELLE. Well, sorta. Then there's Missy Mahoney—

DELMOUNT. Oh, my God! Is she in the pageant?

CARNELLE. Yeah.

DELMOUNT. Why next to her sister, Tessy, Missy's the ugliest girl in the whole town!

43

CARNELLE. Sssh! Sssh! (*Pointing to the dressing room.*) Tessy's in charge of the pageant coordination. She may hear you.

DELMOUNT. Oh, Jesus. Keep me away from those two. They are trouble.

CARNELLE. Well, Tessy was asking about you just now.

DELMOUNT. She was? Holy cow; holy cow. Where's my pipe? I've got to lay low; that's all. Lay low till I can get out of this town for good and always.

CARNELLE. Let's see, then there's Caroline Jeffers. She is awfully pretty except . . . Oh, I don't know! I don't know! (*She begins chewing her nails.*) Have you seen Elain?

DELMOUNT. Not since this morning.

CARNELLE. She was gonna go find Popeye to help sew up that red dress. It looks funny the way it is.

DELMOUNT. Well, I haven't seen Popeye since that night you got into this blessed contest.

CARNELLE. (*Biting her nails.*) Oh, shoot! I said I wasn't gonna chew on my nails! (*She takes a nail file from her dress pocket and begins filing.*)

DELMOUNT. She's strange anyway . . . that Popeye. She's very strange. A strange bird.

CARNELLE. (*Working on her nails.*) I guess so. I guess she is. Still . . . well, I guess, I shouldn't tell you. No, never mind.

DELMOUNT. Oh, that's fine. That's just fine. You start to say something and then you don't. Very nice, Carnelle, very nice.

CARNELLE. Well, it's just . . . it's just, well, she said she liked your hair and —

DELMOUNT. What? My hair? She said she likes my hair?!

CARNELLE. Yes, and how you can wiggle your ears and write poetry.

DELMOUNT. Wiggle my ears!? Good Lord and butter.

CARNELLE. Oh, I may as well tell you . . . she's in love with you.

DELMOUNT. What!?! No, she's not. I don't believe that. Who told you that?

CARNELLE. Well, she said it. And she was crying over you. It's the truth, Delmount. She was in the living room crying over you.

DELMOUNT. No, I don't believe it. Crying?

CARNELLE. I know. But I didn't have the heart to tell her

about your obsessive eye for beauty. You know; that one you have.

DELMOUNT. Oh. Yes, I have acquired a weakness for the classical, exotic beauty in a woman. I've been a fool for it. It's my romantic nature.

CARNELLE. And I guess you don't think that Popeye's exactly classical? (*Delmount looks forlornly at her.*) Well, I've got to at least go put on my pantaloons and hoop. I've got to at least do that.

DELMOUNT. This tobacco is too sweet. It's making my head spin. Anyway, my hair's an unruly mess!

ELAIN'S VOICE. Carnelle! Carnation, Honey!?!

CARNELLE. (*Stopping.*) Elain—(*Elain enters R. in a flowing summer dress. She looks radiant and fresh. She carries the Mardi gras mask in a paper sack.*)

ELAIN. Oh, Da'lin, there you are!

CARNELLE. Oh, Elain, I knew you'd come!

ELAIN. Why, hello, Delly!

DELMOUNT. Hello Swaney.

ELAIN. Will you just look up at that sky! It's as blue as the mighty sea! Oh, I feel like a child today! I swear, I do! You'll never believe it, but Miss Blue has asked me to come up and give a speech before the contest starts. She wants me to talk on, "My Life as a Beauty." Isn't it too exciting!

CARNELLE. Oh, yes, yes. But—but where's Popeye? The dress—I couldn't make it look right.

ELAIN. Oh, Carnation, I went over to Miss Lily's Dress Shop and heard the most disheartening news: poor, little Popeye was fired yesterday afternoon. They said she was giving away the merchandise.

CARNELLE. Oh, no!

DELMOUNT. Well, where'd she go?

ELAIN. No one knows. They haven't seen her. But anyway, I came up with the most creative idea to save the day. You can wear this lovely Mardi gras mask in the opening parade. That way you can just hold it up to your face like this, covering the side of your dress where the extra material is with your arm and elbows, plus adding some mystery and elegance to—well, to your total look. Just walk around like this. (*She moves around making dips and swirls, alternately moving the mask from in front of her face to the side of it with flip of her wrist, as she makes her dips.*) And

45

scoop! And scoop! And scoop! You think you can manage it?
CARNELLE. (*Taking the mask.*) I'll try. I'll really try. (*She begins practicing.*) And scoop! And scoop. And scoop, etc.
ELAIN. That's it. Now just flip out your wrist. Make it crisp! That's good. Just keep at it. That's the only way to improve. (*Turning to Delmount.*) It's amazing but everyone recognizes me. They say I'm still exactly the same as I was. "Just in full bloom like a rose!" That's what one dear man said. I wish Mama were here. She'd love all of this!
CARNELLE. (*Still practicing.*) I know. She'd be so surprised if she could see me. I'm totally changed from when she knew me. Totally new. I think I got it. (*Tessy sticks her head into the* L. *side of the dressing room.*)
TESSY. Carnelle?
CARNELLE. Out here, Tessy! I'm here!
CARNELLE AND ELAIN. Tessy!
DELMOUNT. Tessy! (*He leaps under the tent.*)
TESSY. (*Entering the dressing room* L. *carrying a shoe box with a rubber band around it and holes punched in it.*) Carnelle?!
CARNELLE. I'm over here!
TESSY. Oh! (*As she steps out of the dressing room to the outside area.*) Why, Elain! Hello! How're you doing?
ELAIN. Why, if it isn't Tessy Mahoney! I'm doing fine. Just fine.
TESSY. Will you look at you. If you aren't the most beautiful thing in the whole wide world!
ELAIN. Oh, you silly, dear!
TESSY. (*Handing Carnelle the shoe box.*) Here, Carnelle. Some man brought this as a gift to you.
CARNELLE. Why, thank you. Who could have sent it?
TESSY. I just can't get over how beautiful you are. I just can't.
ELAIN. Why, how sweet can you be?
CARNELLE. (*Reading the scrawled message.*) "Thought you'd enjoy this. Good luck always. Mac Sam."
ELAIN. So, what's in the box?
CARNELLE. I don't know. But I—I think it's alive.
ELAIN. What? Let me see—(*She opens the box.*) AAH!!! (*She slams the top back on the box and drops it to the ground.*)
CARNELLE. What is it?
ELAIN. It's a horrible little frog in a pink outfit!

46

CARNELLE. Oh, my lord. (*She picks up the box and looks inside.*) Oh, lord. (*To Tessy.*) Where'd he go? Where'd the man go?

TESSY. I don't know. He gave me the box up front.

CARNELLE. Show me. Quick! Show me!

TESSY. (*As she hurries back through the dressing room and runs off* L.) Well, it's this way. But you better hurry up; it's only seventeen minutes till the opening Parade of Firecrackers—

CARNELLE. (*Overlapping as she follows Tessy out.*) Come on, Elain! Come on! He'll know where Popeye is! He'll know!

ELAIN. (*Following Carnelle off* L., *overlapping.*) But why? What do you mean? What's all this about? What an awful gift! Some friend you must have! (*They all exit* L. *Delmount comes out from under the tent. He is dusting off his pants when Popeye suddenly enters from down right dancing, humming, and eating blue cotton candy. She is wearing her earbobs and a pretty summer dress.*)

DELMOUNT. Popeye.

POPEYE. (*Stopping her dancing.*) Hello. (*She fans herself with the blue cotton candy as they stare at each other for a moment.*) I was looking for Carnelle.

DELMOUNT. Oh. Well. I don't know. I think she went looking for you. Found some sort of frog in a suit.

POPEYE. Was it a pink suit?

DELMOUNT. I think it was.

POPEYE. Oh, well, I sold me about ten different outfits out at a booth this morning. But I only had me that one frog in the pink suit, kinda there on display; case you didn't have no dolls.

DELMOUNT. I see.

POPEYE. Well. So why was Carnelle a'hunting for me?

DELMOUNT. Oh. Well, she, ah, she needed you to help sew on this red dress she has for the contest. She's been looking for you since last night.

POPEYE. Oh. Well, I rode the bus up to Jackson last night. Went to visit the observatory. They had the telescope aimed up on the moon. Thought I'd take a look.

DELMOUNT. How'd it look?

POPEYE. Big. Orange. Kinda shiney and sparkley.

DELMOUNT. Sounds nice.

POPEYE. It was.

DELMOUNT. (*There is an awkward pause. He begins smoothing down his hair.*) Hmm. Gosh. (*He stops smoothing. Looks at her.*)

47

Oh. (*Suddenly messing his hair all up.*) I prefer it unruly. Don't you?

POPEYE. I don't much know. (*A pause.*) Ah, where's the dress? Maybe I should go take a look at it.

DELMOUNT. Oh, well, it's in here. It's right in here. (*They go inside the dressing room. He shows her the dress.*) It's ah, too small right here in the waist.

POPEYE. Hmm. Let me take a look.

DELMOUNT. Well, here, I'll hold your cotton candy.

POPEYE. Thanks. You can finish it, if you want. (*At that moment Carnelle, Mac Sam, and Elain are heard coming from the carnival from down R. They are in an uproar.*)

MAC SAM'S VOICE. But I told you, I took the thing from some small kid who was tired of it! How do I know where he got it!?!

ELAIN. (*Overlapping.*) Well, in my opinion, it's a tasteless sort of gift! (*By now they are all on stage.*)

MAC SAM. I thought it was festive!! A unique gift for a unique girl! Who are you anyway?!

ELAIN. Who are *you?!?*

DELMOUNT. Wait! It's them! (*Stepping outside the dressing room.*) She's here! She's inside! Popeye! She's looking at the dress!

CARNELLE. She is?!

ELAIN. She's here!?

MAC SAM. Who is this Popeyed anyway? (*They all rush into the dressing room. The following dialogue goes at a rapid pace.*)

CARNELLE. Popeye! You're here!

POPEYE. Hello. I need scissors.

ALL. Scissors. Scissors.

CARNELLE. Scissors. Scissors. Let me look. Let me look! (*She begins searching through her makeup case.*)

DELMOUNT. Listen, Bub, those balloons don't fit in here.

MAC SAM. Is that Popeyed?

ELAIN. Popeye! It's Popeye!

CARNELLE. Oh, I don't think I have any scissors! They're none here!

TESSY'S VOICE. (*Coming from off L.*) Elain! Oh, Miss Elain!

DELMOUNT, ELAIN, CARNELLE. Tessy!

DELMOUNT. Quick! Hide me behind those balloons. (*Delmount jumps behind Mac Sam's balloons.*)

MAC SAM. Watch it, Sonny!

TESSY. (*As she enters from the L. side of the dressing room.*) Miss Blue says it's only five minutes till she introduces you for your speech on beauty.

ELAIN. Oh, thank you, Darlin. Thank you. (*Looking in the mirror.*) For heaven's sake, my face isn't even on!

MAC SAM. Her face?

TESSY. Why, Carnelle, you'd better hurry and get dressed! All the other beauty contestants are already in their gowns and ready to go! (*She exits L., blowing her whistle. All scream. Delmount reappears.*)

CARNELLE. What can I do? There're no scissors. What can I do?!

ELAIN. (*Sitting at the dressing table, putting on her makeup.*) Just wear the mask; you'll be fine, really.

CARNELLE. Oh, will somebody, please, take this frog!?

MAC SAM. Here, Honey, Mac Sam'll take care of it. (*He takes the box from her.*)

CARNELLE. Quick, now my pantaloons! Oh, God, I'm hot. I'm sweating. I stink. (*Someone throws her the pantaloons.*)

DELMOUNT. I believe I mentioned your balloons don't fit!

MAC SAM. I'm holding the frog!

CARNELLE. (*Struggling with her pantaloons.*) Oh! Oh, which is the right end?! Look, I can't even find the right end of my pantaloons! It's hopeless!! It's hopeless!! It's utterly hopeless!! (*She throws the pantaloons into the air, collapses on the floor then starts crawling around on the floor searching for her pantaloons.*)

ELAIN. Now just try to be calm, Carnation, Honey. Try to enjoy yourself; it's all going to go as smooth as silk! I promise you—I give you my word of honor!

DELMOUNT. You'll do alright, Child a Mine—It's a stupid, idiotic contest, you'll do fine!

MAC SAM. You're beautiful, Baby—just beautiful!

POPEYE. (*About the pantaloons.*) Here. Here, now. You step in 'em like this.

MAC SAM. Yeah, put your foot in there.

CARNELLE. (*Trembling.*) In there? Right in there?

POPEYE. Uh huh.

DELMOUNT. Come on, child, you can do it.

CARNELLE. (*Gritting her teeth.*) Well, alright. (*She grabs the pantaloons and furiously starts to put them on.*)

MAC SAM. That's it!

ELAIN. Good. Good.

DELMOUNT. You've got it now!

CARNELLE. Hey! Hey, look, they're on me! My pantaloons are on!! (*General applause, sighs of relief, etc. Mac Sam raises Carnelle's hand in victory. Fast blackout.*)

END OF SCENE

ACT II

Scene Two

The setting is the same. Several minutes have passed. The red dress, the hoop, the pantaloons, and the Mardi gras mask are gone. Mac Sam sits on the bench smoking a cigarette and drinking whiskey from a flask. His balloons are tied to the bench. Delmount is pacing back and forth in front of the bench.

DELMOUNT. Wonder how it's going?

MAC SAM. Why don't ya take a look?

DELMOUNT. Not interested.

MAC SAM. Oh.

DELMOUNT. She look alright to you in that big, red thing?

MAC SAM. Oh, yeah.

DELMOUNT. God. How she can put herself through this I'll never understand. Never.

MAC SAM. Well, women are funny about their looks. My granpapa used to say to me, "Sammy, all ya have to do is tell a woman she's beautiful and she goes like that!" (*He makes a horizontal victory sign with his fingers.*)

DELMOUNT. How pithy.

MAC SAM. Well, of course I try not to abuse the knowledge but it has come in handy in some borderline cases.

DELMOUNT. Well, fortunately, I have yet to make advances

50

to any woman who did not possess at least one classically, beautiful characteristic. It's sort of a romantic notion I've had. I don't know. Perhaps, it's caused me to be fragmented in love. Perhaps, it's been obsessive. What do you think?

MAC SAM. Well, what I like is a woman who can take it right slap on the chin. That's what I like. (*He begins to cough, spreading germs all over his flask. He takes a slug, relieving his cough, then he says.*) Care for a slug?

DELMOUNT. (*Aghast.*) No, thank you. (*Popeye and Elain enter in a flurry from up* R. *Popeye carries a half eaten hot dog.*)

POPEYE. Ooh! Ooh, me! Ooh!

ELAIN. (*Overlapping.*) It's a travesty! A travesty! An utter God-forsake travesty!

DELMOUNT. What's going on? Is it going alright? How's it going?

ELAIN. Air! Air! I must have some air! (*She falls back onto the bench as Delmount and Mac Sam fan her furiously.*)

POPEYE. (*Acting it out.*) See, see, she tripped on that big ole red skirt and fell down flat on her face! Whoops! (*She falls to the ground.*) And people was laughing. 'Ha, ha, ha, ha, ha!'

DELMOUNT. (*Overlapping.*) Laughing! Oh, my God! Laughing!

POPEYE. They was laughing out loud!

ELAIN. (*Coming out of her faint.*) There — there's a group of hoodlums out there yelling, "Miss Hot Tamale! Miss Hot Tamale!!" It's a disgrace. It's a humiliation! And that horrible Ronnie Wayne is actually throwing peanuts and trash and ice right up there on the stage in front of everyone!

DELMOUNT. At her? Is he throwing them at her?

ELAIN. Well, a peanut caught her right between the eyes!

DELMOUNT. What? What! He dies!! DIES!!!! Ronnie Wayne! Ronnie Wayne!! (*Delmount exits* U.R. *as Carnelle enters* L. *into her dressing room. The red dress, which was quite lovely and seductive when Elain wore it eleven years ago, now looks like a whore's gown on Carnelle. It is faded and ill fitted and totally askew. She slings down the torn and broken Mardi gras mask furiously. There are peanuts and trash on her dress and in her hair.*)

CARNELLE. AAAAH! OOH! It's awful! It's so awful! They never forget! They never do! (*Elain and Popeye start for the dressing room. Mac Sam stays on the bench. He lights up another cigarette.*)

51

ELAIN. (*Overlapping.*) It's her! She's there!! (*Stepping inside the dressing room.*) Carnation—

POPEYE. (*Stepping inside.*) Hi.

CARNELLE. Did you hear them? Oh, did you hear them? They were laughing and calling me, "Miss Hot Tamale." Did you hear it?

ELAIN. Why, look at you, you're dripping wet . . . let me help you out of this gown before you perish. (*She starts to unbutton the gown.*)

CARNELLE. Oh, if only the dress had come sooner. I could have fixed it right. I wouldn't of needed that fancy mask. I felt so foolish wearing it.

ELAIN. (*Defensively, as she tries to get the dress over Carnelle's head.*) I'm sorry, but I thought it would do—I just didn't realize that, well, that you were so big boned! Anyway, the color's all wrong—it was just too loud.

CARNELLE. But I love the color red. I love how it blazes!! Oh, I've got a pushing sensation right between my eyes as though it like to crack open my brains! Ooh!!

ELAIN. Now, listen, Carnation, if you don't calm down, you're headed for a clear cut nervous breakdown! Just try to remember how Mama was enlightened by her affliction. Why, remember what she was always telling you, "Pretty is as pretty does." (*Carnelle collapses in despair.*)

POPEYE. You want this hot dog? I ain't enjoying it.

CARNELLE. Thanks. (*Carnelle takes the hot dog and stuffs it into her mouth, as Tessy enters L. She is in an uproar.*)

TESSY. Will you stop him! Will you please try and stop him!! He's messing up Missy's whole opus. He's out there in the audience causing a horrible, horrible scene!!

CARNELLE. (*Overlapping.*) Who? What? Stop who?!

TESSY. Delmount, that's who! He's smashing Ronnie Wayne's head into the dirt! And everyone's hollering!

CARNELLE. Oh, Lord, I've got to stop him—(*She starts to leave L.*)

TESSY. No! Don't go through the stage!

CARNELLE. Oh—(*She turns and runs out the R. side of the dressing room.*)

ELAIN. Wait! Carnelle! You're in your hoop!

52

CARNELLE. (*Who is now in the outside area.*) Oh, no! I'm in my hoop!

MAC SAM. Well, you don't have to tell me!

CARNELLE. (*Covering herself.*) Oh, please, run around there and stop Delmount! He's out there in a fight — he's stirring up trouble!

MAC SAM. Alright, Baby. I'm going. (*About his balloons.*) Hey, see that no one steals my capital! (*He exits up* R.)

CARNELLE. Thanks, Mac Sam! Thanks a lot! (*She goes back into the dressing room.*) It's alright. It'll be fine. Mac Sam's gone to stop him.

TESSY. That Delmount is just wild. He is just recklessly wild!

ELAIN. (*Sitting down on a stool, fanning herself.*) Well, as we all know, he's had a very checkered past. (*Tessy looks to Elain who turns away with a grimace.*)

TESSY. I suppose, Missy's whole opus is just ruined. Well, be that as it may, the show must go on. (*Looking at her clipboard.*) Let's see . . . let me get this straight. Joe Anne Jacobs follows Missy with her comedy pantomine to, "Take Me Out to the Ball Game," then ther'll be Caroline Jeffers' dramatic interpretation from, *Gone With the Wind.* Then, of course, there's Saphire's holla hoop act and finally, last but not least, is your tap dance routine to, "The Star Spangled Banner." Alright, do you have that order?

CARNELLE. (*Who has removed her hoop and put on a robe.*) Uh huh.

TESSY. Since you go on last, it looks like you'll have to really rush to get into that bathing suit for the final crowning.

CARNELLE. It doesn't matter. It's all over. It's all ruined.

ELAIN. Don't worry, we'll help her out. It won't be a problem.

TESSY. Why, thank you, Elain. You're probably the most admirable person I've ever met. Truly you are! Oh my! (*She exits* L.)

ELAIN. It's sweltering in here. Let's get some air. (*She steps from the dressing room to the outside area.*)

CARNELLE. (*Following her.*) Alright.

POPEYE. Good. Maybe we can catch a breeze. (*She steps outside the dressing room.*)

CARNELLE. I hope so, Popeye. Oh lord. I do.

DELMOUNT'S VOICE. I showed them! I showed them all!!
Those cold blooded swine!! (*Mac Sam and Delmount appear from*
U.R. *Mac Sam is supporting Delmount who is dragging his leg and has*
blood on his face.)
POPEYE. Oh!!
CARNELLE. Delmount!
ELAIN. Delly, are you alright?!
CARNELLE. What's happened?
MAC SAM. They started throwing rocks at him. They hit him
there on the leg.
CARNELLE. Oh, Lord, are you hurt? You're not hurt are
you?!
DELMOUNT. They don't make um hard enough.
ELAIN. Well, you look dreadful. I'll run get that disinfectant
from the car! (*She exits* D.R.)
POPEYE. Well, I'll—I'll get ya some ice. You can put it on
your swolled up leg! (*She exits down* R.)
CARNELLE. (*Sinking to the ground.*) This is awful. Throwing
rocks. They were throwing rocks. I'm about to cry.
DELMOUNT. It's alright, Child a mine. Nobody's hurt. We
enjoyed it.
MAC SAM. Yeah. (*Cough, cough.*) Yeah. (*Cough, cough, cough,*
cough, cough. He spits up blood.)
CARNELLE. Mac Sam, what's wrong? Are you choking?
MAC SAM. Nah. I'm just spitting up clots of blood.
CARNELLE. What?
MAC SAM. It's nothing. Happens all the time. Look at that
clot there; it's a nice pinkish-reddish sorta color.
CARNELLE. You're making me sick, here. Sick. (*Tessy enters*
L. *into the dressing room. She is holding a record.*)
TESSY. Carnelle?! Oh Carnelle!
CARNELLE. It's Tessy.
DELMOUNT. Christ, I'm too weak to move.
TESSY. (*Stepping outside, spotting Delmount.*) Why, will you look
at you! I just hope you're proud of yourself. Causing all of that
racket! Here, Carnelle, Tommy Turner wants you to show him
which song on this record you want played for your routine.
CARNELLE. Alright. (*She takes the record, goes through the dressing*
room and exits L.)

54

TESSY. So how's life been treating you?

DELMOUNT. Oh, fair.

TESSY. Well, I just thought you should know that I'm still bearing emotional scars because of the time you took unfair advantage of me up in the attic. They're deep scars, Delmount. They hurt.

DELMOUNT. (*Quietly as he squirms.*) Have a little mercy. I'm bleeding here. Look: blood. (*He mops off his head with a handkerchief.*)

TESSY. Well, you don't have to worry. I've already forgiven you. It's my religion: First Presbyterian. And to show you I mean it, tonight I'll let you take me to watch the fireworks.

DELMOUNT. What—

TESSY. (*She starts to leave.*) I'll even trust you to sit by me all alone in the dark! See you back here at 7:45 p.m. on the nose!

DELMOUNT. No, wait—(*He tries to get up but flinches in pain.*)

TESSY. (*As she exits through the dressing room and out L.*) I've got to run now! There's a show on!

DELMOUNT. (*Overlapping, he crawls after her.*) Please—Don't forgive me! Don't forgive me! Don't! It was rotten behavior! I stink, I tell ya! I stink! (*Dropping to the ground.*) Christ.

MAC SAM. (*After a moment.*) Classically—beautiful—characteristics?

DELMOUNT. She was an exception.

MAC SAM. I'll say.

DELMOUNT. It was a long time ago.

MAC SAM. You don't have to make excuses to me. I've done nearly as bad myself. Course, now, Alligator Woman did have a way with her tongue. (*He helps Delmount to the bench as Popeye enters from D.R. She carries a purple snow cone.*)

DELMOUNT. All right! All right! So I'm confused about women. I'm an idiot! A fool!

MAC SAM. Relax, chump. I'm just enjoying the day.

POPEYE. Here! Here, I got ya some ice. It oughta help take down that swelling.

DELMOUNT. But that's purple ice!

POPEYE. Well, they was out a cherry.

MAC SAM. Hmm. That's pretty good, Popeye! Pretty good! Here, pull up the pants. (*He jerks up Delmount's pants leg.*)

DELMOUNT. AAH!

MAC SAM. (*Taking the snow cone and dumps it down on Delmount's leg.*) Now slap down that ice!

DELMOUNT. Jesus Christ, Man!!

MAC SAM. Feel better? (*Elain enters from* D.R. *She carries a can of medicated spray.*)

ELAIN. I'm back, Delly! I'm back! You can just relax now! You're gonna be fine! Let me just put on this medicated spray —

DELMOUNT. Look, it's all right. I'm fine. I don't need anything *else.*

ELAIN. Oh, my God! Your leg's turned purple! I think I'm gonna faint!

DELMOUNT. No, it's ice! Purple ice! (*Holding up the paper cone.*) Ice!

ELAIN. Oh! Well, you had me going. For awhile there, you did have me going. Now let me just apply this spray —

DELMOUNT. Look, I'm fine! I don't need anything else; so just leave me alone. *Okay?*

ELAIN. Well, alright. Alright. You can't do anything with him when he gets like this. (*Her eyes meet Mac Sam's.*) Hello.

MAC SAM. (*Saying everything with his magnetic eyes.*) Hello.

ELAIN. (*Nervously.*) So, Popeye, we hear you, ah, lost your job.

POPEYE. Well, I was fired from it.

ELAIN. It's such a shame.

DELMOUNT. Yeah. It is.

ELAIN. (*Primarily for Mac Sam's benefit.*) So, what transpired? I mean, what all happened? Do tell!

POPEYE. Oh, well, I reckon what it was was when I was sewing up there in the front a the big store. This little child walked in and she started looking in at all that shiny jewelry behind the glass counter. I saw her looking and I said, 'My, what lovely eyes you have. Them's pretty eyes. What color are them eyes?' And she looks up at me and say, 'I don't know. I don't have no idea.'

ELAIN. Imagine, not knowing the color of your own eyes. Amazing. Continue, please.

POPEYE. Well, I gets out this compact case from behind the glass counter. It's covered with the most beautiful colored sea shells in all the world. And I give it to her and says, "Look in there and tell me what color your eyes is." She takes a long look and says, "Them's blue eyes." And that was the truth, she was right about it. So I give her the sea shelled compact case to take on with her, just by chance she forgets what color her eyes is and needs to take a look. Well, Miss Celia Lilly comes looking for that compact case later on in the day. I told her what happened and that's when she give me the news, "Popeye, you're fired."

MAC SAM. Hey. I like this Popeye character. She's hep.

DELMOUNT. Hep? She isn't hep.

ELAIN. Well, it's a shame, Popeye. They should have given you a second chance.

POPEYE. Oh, I don't mind it. I like traveling. (*About Mac Sam who is casually blowing out smoke rings.*) Hey, look! He's blowing smoke rings out from his mouth! Watch him! Wooh! What a trick!

MAC SAM. (*Taking the cigarette out of his mouth.*) Oh, that — that's nothing. Here, take a look at this! (*As he sticks the lit part of his cigarette into his mouth.*) Enter the infernal jaws of hell! (*With the backwards cigarette in his mouth, he blows out smoke.*)

POPEYE. Oh, look! Smoke! He's blowing out smoke! He's gonna burn up his throat!!!

MAC SAM. (*Taking out the cigarette. To Popeye.*) Ta! Da! How'd ya like that, Beautiful? (*Delmount's eyes go crazy.*)

POPEYE. It was wonderful! It was!! Do you know anymore?

DELMOUNT. Here! I know one! I can do one. Just watch! Now I'm going to wiggle my ears!

ELAIN. Oh, that's right! Delmount can do the most stupendous trick where he wiggles his ears!

POPEYE. Oh, let's see it! (*They all watch as Delmount makes a facial grimace, while trying to wiggle his ears.*)

MAC SAM. (*After a moment.*) I don't see em wiggling.

ELAIN. No, they're not wiggling.

POPEYE. Nah, they ain't.

DELMOUNT. Well, I — guess I'm out of practice. (*Mac Sam laughs cheerfully.*)

POPEYE. (*Disappointed.*) Ooh.

DELMOUNT. But here, I can do this trick where my thumb comes off. Like this! (*He does the trick where his thumb comes off.*)

POPEYE. Oh, I know that one too! (*She takes off her thumb.*)

ELAIN. That's an old one. (*She takes off her thumb.*)

MAC SAM. Yeah. (*He takes off his.*)

DELMOUNT. Well, perhaps I should just go! . . . I don't know. I don't know. (*He wanders away from the group. Carnelle enters L. into the dressing room.*)

CARNELLE. (*Mumbling to herself, as she sinks down at the dressing table.*) "I'll never be hungry again. I'll never be hungry again. As God is my witness . . . As God is my witness . . ."

POPEYE. (*Spotting Carnelle through the doorway.*) Carnelle! Is it time for your act to go on? (*Running inside the dressing room.*) Do you need some help?

CARNELLE. Oh, Popeye, I was just watching Caroline Jeffers do that heartbreaking speech from, *Gone With the Wind,* — I tell you, that's what I should have done: a dramatic interpretation piece. See, because I could break down and cry real tears right now if I wanted too. It's acting like I was laughing or happy or something — that's what'd be hard.

POPEYE. I like you act. It's beautiful. Them roman candles shooting off. Here, put on your suit. (*She hands Carnelle the red, blue and silver costume.*)

ELAIN. (*To Mac Sam.*) So, Mr. Mac Sam, what sort of day have you been having?

MAC SAM. Oh, not bad. Just been sitting here rotting away in the July sun.

DELMOUNT. (*Walking up to them.*) Excuse me. I believe I need to apply some medical spray to my wounds. (*He takes the spray and moves away.*)

POPEYE. (*About Carnelle's costume.*) Oh, that looks so good. Them silver stars really shine.

CARNELLE. I don't know, Popeye. I'm afraid it's a lost cause.

POPEYE. But I love it when you twirl them sparklers all around. I practically lose my breath. Here're your tap shoes.

ELAIN. Nice assortment of balloons you've got — and in a variety of colors.

MAC SAM. And which may I ask, is your favorite color?

ELAIN. Pink. I adore, pink.

MAC SAM. Ah, pink. I once knew a woman whose skin was awfully pink and pretty looking.

DELMOUNT. (*Sticking his head into the dressing room.*) Hey, what does that guy do? He looks like a corpse. How does he look like that?

CARNELLE. He's sick.

DELMOUNT. I'll buy that. (*He leaves.*)

POPEYE. Gosh. I've been trying so hard t'forget him.

CARNELLE. You mean, Delmount?

POPEYE. Uh huh.

CARNELLE. How's it going?

POPEYE. Well, today I found out he'd forgotten how t'wiggle his ears. But it don't matter.

TESSY'S VOICE. Carnelle! (*Tessy enters the dressing room* L.) They're voting on Saphire's hoolahoop act right now! You better get out there. You're on next! (*She blows her whistle and exits* L.)

CARNELLE. Oh, my God, I'm on next. I'm next.

POPEYE. (*Running outside.*) Hey, everyone! Carnelle's on next! She's gonna be doing her dancing routine to, "The Star Spangled Banner!"

MAC SAM. (*Getting up and making his exit* U.R.) I'm on my way!

CARNELLE. I don't know if I can go back out there.

POPEYE. Here's your sparklers and your roman candle.

CARNELLE. Do I look okay?

POPEYE. Just right.

CARNELLE. Let's go. (*They exit* L.)

ELAIN. Well, aren't you going?

DELMOUNT. I don't think I can watch it. I mean, she thinks she's tap dancing and she's just clomping her feet around. It makes me very anxious.

ELAIN. Poor, Carnation. She wants to be beautiful without understanding the limitations it brings.

DELMOUNT. Well, it'll all be over soon. Carnelle will go up to Memphis; I'll start my life in New Orleans and you'll go— wherever the winds take you. (*He looks over at Elain who seems somber.*) Hey, don't worry, Swayne. You're free. You're finally gonna find out just why you're alive. (*Tessy enters* L. *She carries a box of long-stemmed roses and brings them out to Elain.*)

TESSY. Elain! Oh, Elain! Look, here's a box of flowers that were sent to you. Isn't it exciting! Oh, here's the card; it dropped off. (*She hands the card to Delmount because Elain is holding the box.*)

Well, I've got to rush back! Got a show on! Don't forget the fireworks! (*She exits through the dressing room and off* L.)

DELMOUNT. I thought he stopped sending the roses.

ELAIN. He did.

DELMOUNT. Mind if I take a look at this card?

ELAIN. Go ahead.

DELMOUNT. "My Dear Elain, I've been very, very happy since your phone call this morning. How I do need to hear how much you love me. I'll be by for you tomorrow morning at eleven a.m. You're adoring husband, Franklin." (*After a moment.*) What kind of idiot am I? What kind of dupe? You would think that after you left me in that lunatic asylum I would know not to trust you.

ELAIN. Be fair! You always had everything! Mama left the whole of the house to you and all of the furniture and all of the silver and even the handmade quilts! She left nothing to me! Nothing at all!

DELMOUNT. You can have it. You can have all of the money that's made! Just leave him.

ELAIN. (*Overlapping.*) I don't want it. Stop planning my life! I'm used to better things now . . . my face cream . . . my clocks. And he adores me. I need someone who adores me. (*Mac Sam enters U.R. in excitement.*)

MAC SAM. (*Throwing a handful of confetti.*) Stupendous! Ravishing! A little bit of sheer heaven!

ELAIN. What—(*Carnelle and Popeye enter the dressing room* L. *They are elated. Carnelle twirls a burning sparkler.*)

CARNELLE. I don't believe it! I don't believe it! They were all clapping! It was a hit!

POPEYE. (*Overlapping, as she shoots off imaginary Roman candles.*) Pow! Pow! Pow!

MAC SAM. She was out there just dancing and marching and the music was swelling—

POPEYE. (*Overlapping.*) She was so beautiful!

CARNELLE. (*Overlapping as she tap dances and twirls her baton.*) Yes sir! Yes sir!

MAC SAM. (*Running on.*) And everyone started cheering when the Roman candles went off—

POPEYE. Pow! Pow! Zoweey!

CARNELLE. They were cheering for me!

MAC SAM. Brilliant performance! And can she dance! (*Delmount looks dumbfounded.*)

ELAIN. (*Running to join Carnelle and Popeye in the dressing room.*) Did it really go well? Did it really?

POPEYE. Oh brother! I about died!

CARNELLE. Quick! Let's go girls! I gotta change into my bathing suit! I don't have much time.

MAC SAM. (*Sitting down.*) Boy, (*cough, cough*) so beautiful, (*cough, cough, cough*) so fine!

DELMOUNT. (*Accusingly.*) Tell me, just exactly what do you mean when you're telling Carnelle how beautiful she is?

MAC SAM. I mean she's . . . beautiful.

DELMOUNT. You're a liar.

MAC SAM. Yeah, well, I do work the carnivals. (*He spits up a clot of blood.*)

CARNELLE. (*Pulling up her bathing suit.*) Lord, is this tight! Come on. There! There, I got it. I hope this French bra'll help. How do my thighs look?

TESSY. (*Sticking her head into the room* L.) Quick! Get out there! They're starting the lineup! (*She exits* L. *blowing her whistle.*)

CARNELLE. Oh, my God. It's time for the final crowning. It's time! Hey, let me wave goodbye to the boys. (*Carnelle waves goodbye.*) Goodbye, boys! I'm going. I'm going out to the final crowning!

MAC SAM. Hey—good luck! We'll be right there cheering!

DELMOUNT. You look good, Child!

ELAIN. Do your best.

CARNELLE. (*Hugging them.*) Oh, Elain! Oh, Popeye!

TESSY. (*Sticking her head in.*) Come on! Their moving out on the stage!

CARNELLE. Farewell, Everyone! Farewell! (*Carnelle exits* L.)

POPEYE. Quick! We've got t'run around and see her! (*She starts out.*)

MAC SAM. I'm moving out! (*Elain pauses a moment to exchange a look with Delmount. She then turns and exits. Delmount looks after them. He paces around for several moments. He glances into the empty dressing room.*)

DELMOUNT. I'll never understand it. Never. It lacks sense. It makes me ill. I mean, for Christ's sake who would want to ride in a parade? It's so pitiful. Man parading his ridiculous pomposity down his pathetic little streets, cheering at his own inane self-grandeur. (*He looks at himself in the dressing room mirror.*) Oh, God I hope she comes in first! I hope she does. I do. I do. I swear I hope she beats them all!! (*Mac Sam enters* U.R.)

MAC SAM. Wooh. Amazing. Unbelievable. (*Delmount looks at him.*) She lost. I don't know what for.

DELMOUNT. Holy cow. Holy cow. (*Elain and Popeye enter* U.R.)

ELAIN. Oh! I just don't understand it. She tries so hard. I guess, they really just took those, "Miss Hot Tamales," to heart. (*To Delmount.*) Did you hear the results?

DELMOUNT. I heard.

ELAIN. Course everyone knew Caroline Jeffers would come in first. And I suppose, in a way, it's understandable that Joe Anne came in second.

DELMOUNT. The shrimp?

ELAIN. But, I mean, when Missy Mahoney came in third!

DELMOUNT. Third!

ELAIN. Well, I nearly died! But to me the crowning blow was having Saphire Mendoza come in ahead of our Carnation! That was the crowning blow!

DELMOUNT. Holy cow. What are we gonna say to her? What are we gonna say? (*Carnelle enters the dressing room* L. *They all stare at her. She wears a fifth place banner. She looks at herself in the mirror, then she bravely turns to face her family and friends, hoping for acceptance.*) Well, it was a stupid meaningless contest.

MAC SAM. Completely laughable.

ELAIN. Mama always said that what's really important in life is—

CARNELLE. I—don't—want—to—hear—it!! I wanted to win that contest. I cared about it. It was important to me. (*To Delmount.*) And I don't care how stupid and meaningless you think it was!! (*To Elain.*) And what are you looking at?! You never wanted me to win! You think I'm ugly that's why you told me to wear that stupid mask over my face! I can't believe I ever wanted to be like you or that mean old monkey either! (*Mac Sam starts to cough. Carnelle turns to him.*) And why don't you get well!?! You make me *sick* you're so *sick!!* You look like shit!!! I

62

tell you, I'm so mad I could spit! (*Spit.*) There! (*Spit, spit.*) There, I spit! (*Spit.*) Die you monkey! Die!

TESSY. Carnelle!! (*She enters the dressing room* L. *carying a large American flag on a pole.*) Carnelle, come on! You and Saphire are gonna follow along behind the Grand Float carrying these American flags. You better get out there; everyone's waiting. (*She holds out the large American flag.*)

CARNELLE. (*Grabbing the flag.*) Thanks!

DELMOUNT. Wait. You don't have to do that. You don't have to follow that float.

CARNELLE. Look, if you come in last, you follow that float. I took a chance and I came in last; so, by God, I'm gonna follow that float!! (*She exits* R. *carrying the American flag.*)

MAC SAM. Hey! You're beautiful when you're mad. Beautiful, Baby!

DELMOUNT. She's gonna fall flat on her face carrying that big ole flag.

ELAIN. (*Straight front.*) I'm not like Mama. I'm not.

TESSY. (*Checking her stopwatch.*) Only four hours and forty-nine minutes till tonight's colorful display of fireworks. (*She hurries back into the dressing room and exits* L. *Delmount looks after her, then looks forlornly to Mac Sam. Mac Sam offers his flask — Delmount takes a long slug. Meanwhile, Popeye slowly turns her head upward to look towards the coming fireworks.*)

QUICK FADE TO BLACKOUT
END OF SCENE TWO

ACT II

SCENE THREE

The setting is the same. It is now early evening and darkness is beginning to fall. The stage is empty for a moment then Elain enters the dressing room left. She carries her purse and a half empty bottle of red wine. She is weary and a bit drunk.

63

ELAIN. Carnelle? Good; not here. (*She looks around the empty dressing room then goes and sits down at the dressing table. She gazes at her face in the mirror. She straightens her hair.*) You're not yourself today. Not yourself.

DELMOUNT'S VOICE. Carnelle! Carnelle, you here? Honey? (*He enters L. and spots Elain.*) Oh. Has Carnelle come back yet?

ELAIN. I don't know. I haven't seen her since she ran off and hid after the parade.

DELMOUNT. Think she'll be all right?

ELAIN. I doubt it.

DELMOUNT. Lord, you waiting here for her?

ELAIN. No. I just came by to get my dress. (*She rises and starts gathering up the red dress.*) I don't think she's that interested in seeing me. Looks like she doesn't admire me so much anymore.

DELMOUNT. I don't understand you. I know you're probably a kind person. You gave Popeye your earrings; you have a need to be excited by life. So why do you go back to being what Mama wanted? You know she was mean!

ELAIN. (*Turning to him angrily.*) Yes, I know she was mean and you know it too. So why do you straighten your wild hair? Why do you have horrible, sickening dreams about pieces of women's bodies? Some all beautiful; some all mutilated and bloody! I hate those dreams. I wish you didn't tell me about them. They scare me.

DELMOUNT. I'm sorry. I'm sorry.

ELAIN. It's okay.

DELMOUNT. I—I don't have those dreams anymore. I've stopped having them.

ELAIN. You have?

DELMOUNT. Yes.

ELAIN. Well, good. That's good. Do you want some wine?

DELMOUNT. Sure. Give me some wine. (*She hands him the bottle—he takes a drink. He hands the bottle back to her—she takes a long drink.*)

ELAIN. You know about those earrings I gave Popeye . . .

DELMOUNT. Yeah?

ELAIN. I hated the damn things. They pinched my ears. I was glad to get rid of them.

DELMOUNT. (*After a moment.*) Swayne.

ELAIN. What?

DELMOUNT. You're incredible.

ELAIN. Well, you've always forgiven me.

DELMOUNT. Yeah. I always have.

ELAIN. So I better be going.

DELMOUNT. Where're you going?

ELAIN. (*Referring to the red dress.*) To take this out to the car. Then on out to have some real fun before I drop dead off this planet. I've got myself a date for the fireworks. I'm meeting him in the grove down under the wisteria trees.

DELMOUNT. Well, Honey, I hope you have yourself a real good ole time.

ELAIN. Don't you worry. I'm gonna be a reckless girl at least once in my dreary, dreary life. Bye, bye now. (*She leaves the dressing room. He follows her to the doorway.*)

DELMOUNT. Bye.

ELAIN. (*As she exits down* R., *carrying the red dress.*) Be seeing you!

DELMOUNT. Bye. (*He stands looking after her. Popeye enters* L. *from the dressing room. She wears binoculars around her neck and is eating peanuts from a sack. Turning to see her.*) Popeye —

POPEYE. Hi.

DELMOUNT. Hello.

POPEYE. Is Carnelle come back?

DELMOUNT. No. I'm waiting here for her.

POPEYE. Oh.

DELMOUNT. I'd like to see her.

POPEYE. Yeah.

DELMOUNT. Course, I'm not even sure if she's coming back here or what.

POPEYE. Oh. (*Uneasy, she starts to leave.*)

DELMOUNT. Would you like to wait here too?

POPEYE. (*Stopping.*) Sure. Alright. Peanut?

DELMOUNT. Thanks. (*A pause.*) So you'll be leaving Brookhaven?

POPEYE. I reckon.

DELMOUNT. It's funny cause I'm leaving here too.

POPEYE. You is? Where was you planning to go?

DELMOUNT. I thought I'd be going to New Orleans — get back to the University and learn to be a philosopher. That way, after I have time to study and think it all through, I'll be able to let everyone know why we're living. It'll be a great relief . . . I believe. And where are you going to go?

POPEYE. Well, I don't know the particulars. But I heard a this place name of Elysian fields.

DELMOUNT. Elysian fields?

POPEYE. Right. See, they got this ambrosia t'eat and wine and honey t'drink and all sorts of people carrying on. Do you know what state it's located in?

DELMOUNT. It — isn't in a state.

POPEYE. It ain't?

DELMOUNT. No. It isn't even in the world. It's — it's fictional. It's a made up place. Why it's only in books and stories.

POPEYE. Oh. Well, shoot. Guess I won't be going there. (*Tessy enters* L. *into the dressing room. She is wearing a big straw hat.*)

TESSY. Oh, Delmount!! Are you here? Delmount?! (*She steps from the dressing room to the outside area.*) Oh, there you are! (*Looking at her watch.*) Right on the nose! You punctual thing! Do you like this hat?

DELMOUNT. It becomes you.

TESSY. Isn't he sweet. Well, do come on. Well. Tell your friend good-bye and let's head to the fireworks.

DELMOUNT. Ah, Tessy . . .

TESSY. Yes?

DELMOUNT. Well, I — I can't go with you to the fireworks.

TESSY. Oh, you can't?

DELMOUNT. No, I — I promised Popeye I'd go with her. I'm sorry. I tried to tell you this afternoon.

TESSY. I see. I see. I try to turn the other cheek and you slap it too. You're ungrateful and unworthy and low and dirty and mean! Why, I'm never gonna forgive you again! Never! I hope you rot in H!! (*She exits down* R.)

DELMOUNT. Brother.

POPEYE. Why did you lie t'her?

DELMOUNT. Huh?

POPEYE. You told her you was promised t'go t'the fireworks with me.

DELMOUNT. Oh. Well, I just didn't want to go out to the fireworks with her and . . . And you can't go around obliging other people in this world.

POPEYE. Oh.

DELMOUNT. Of course I do want to go watch the fireworks. They always have a nice, colorful display. You weren't planning to — I don't know, go to the fireworks yourself?

POPEYE. Sure. It's why I brung my binoculars. Had me a place picked out and everything.

DELMOUNT. Oh. Hmm. Well, I guess you . . .

POPEYE. Huh?

DELMOUNT. No, nothing. I'll be seeing you. Bye. (*He exits down* R. *Popeye sits on the bench and stares ahead. She reaches into her peanut bag. There are none left.*)

POPEYE. (*Miserably.*) Guess that's the last of em. (*Delmount reappears abruptly from* D.R.)

DELMOUNT. Popeye would you mind going to watch the fireworks with me tonight?

POPEYE. No. I wouldn't. Sure. Alright.

DELMOUNT. (*Overlapping.*) Good. Good then. Good. Let's go! (*They exit* D.R. *The stage is empty for a moment before Carnelle sneaks on from under the tent. She is wearing a short trench coat over her red bathing suit. She looks around, sees no one and heads into the dressing room. Mac Sam suddenly appears out of the darkness.*)

MAC SAM. Hey! Red! Where ya going?

CARNELLE. Mac Sam! Dammit! I didn't want anyone to see me.

MAC SAM. Well, I saw ya. How ya been?

CARNELLE. Oh, alright.

MAC SAM. Hey, you sure blew up this afternoon.

CARNELLE. I know it.

MAC SAM. Well, you really did explode.

CARNELLE. I know. I'd never been so mad as I was. And I spit out at everyone. I just spit at them Oh! That's so awful it's almost funny!

MAC SAM. Hell, it was the best part of it!

CARNELLE. Oh, I don't know. I better get my stuff out of here.

MAC SAM. You know, I went looking for you after the parade. Where'd you get off to?

CARNELLE. Oh, nowhere. Just out walking by the railroad tracks.

MAC SAM. What were you doing down there?

CARNELLE. (*As she gathers up her belongings.*) Kicking rocks. Thinking. I thought maybe I was a victim of broken dreams but then I thought maybe I wasn't. I was trying so hard t'belong all my life and . . . I don't know. Oh, looks like Elain came for her red dress. Anyway, I just don't know what you can, well, reasonably hope for in life.

MAC SAM. Not much, Baby, not too damn much.

CARNELLE. But something—

MAC SAM. Sure. There's always eternal grace.

CARNELLE. It'd be nice. (*Holding up the shoe box.*) Look, here, my frog's gone.

MAC SAM. Yeah. That Popeye set it loose.

CARNELLE. Oh, well, I still have the suit. (*She holds up the pink suit. They look at each other and smile.*)

MAC SAM. God, you're beautiful. I wouldn't trade those times we had together not for anything.

CARNELLE. (*Throwing her arms around him.*) Really?

MAC SAM. Not for a golden monkey.

CARNELLE. But how about—I mean I gave you—

MAC SAM. Oh, the syph. Hell, I've got t.b., alcoholics disease, rotting gut. I tell ya, I'm having fun taking bets on which part of me'll decay first: the liver, the lungs, the stomach, or the brain.

CARNELLE. (*Suddenly uneasy.*) It's getting late. I gotta go. (*Carnelle leaves the dressing room carrying all of her belongings. He follows.*)

MAC SAM. Hey, listen, you want to go to the fireworks with ole, Mac Sam? We could spend a fine night together.

CARNELLE. No. I—I just need some rest. You'd be tiring me out awful fast.

MAC SAM. Yeah.

CARNELLE. I gotta get this out to the car. Goodbye, Mac Sam. Goodnight. (*He doffs his cap to her. She exits* D.R.)

MAC SAM. Goodbye, Baby. I'll always remember you as the one who could take it on the chin. (*He looks after her a moment, spits up a clot of blood, wipes off his mouth and starts to exit* U.R.) Ah, well, on to the wisteria trees. (*He is gone. Suddenly Popeye and Delmount appear climbing out onto the roof of the tent from off* R. *Popeye is leading; she carries a box of popcorn. Delmount follows nervously.*)

POPEYE. This way. That's right. Hold on, now.

DELMOUNT. Holy Christ.

POPEYE. There. Aren't these seats great?

DELMOUNT. Oh, yeah, wonderful.

POPEYE. And we can keep an eye out for Carnelle — case she comes back by.

DELMOUNT. Yeah. Great.

POPEYE. Here. Take a look through the binoculars. See how the sky looks. (*Delmount looks through the binoculars.*) Well, how's it look?

DELMOUNT. (*Becoming interested.*) Hmm. Not bad.

POPEYE. (*As she throws handfuls of popcorn in front of the binoculars.*) Watch out! It's snowing! Look! It's snowing! See it! See it snowing!

DELMOUNT. (*Overlapping.*) Oh, great! Snow flakes! Yeah! I see it! (*Impulsively, as he takes the binoculars from in front of his eyes.*) Oh, Popeye, I just have to tell you about these beautiful dreams — I just have to — No, it's absurd! (*He turns away in anguish and spots Carnelle who has entered* D.R.) Why, Carnelle!

POPEYE. Oh, Carnelle! Hi!

CARNELLE. (*Taken aback.*) Why look at you two! What in the world are you doing way up there?!

POPEYE. We're gonna watch the fireworks! Come on up!

DELMOUNT. Yeah, come on! Please, we've been missing you. It's great up here!

CARNELLE. No, I really don't care about the fireworks. I think I'm gonna just go on home.

POPEYE. Oh, please, they's so beautiful to see!

DELMOUNT. Come on, Child! Just for awhile. You can come up for awhile.

CARNELLE. No, really, I just left something in the dressing room; I'm gonna get it and go on home. (*She enters the dressing room.*)

DELMOUNT. Lord, I hope she's alright. She didn't even mention the contest. God, I wish she'd come watch the fireworks with us.

POPEYE. Me too. (*Carnelle pulls the artificial dog out from under the dressing table. She pats it.*)

DELMOUNT. Here, you want to look through the binoculars for awhile?

POPEYE. Okay. (*Popeye takes the binoculars and looks through them.*

69

Carnelle sits at the dressing table and looks at herself in the mirror.) Ooh, I love the heavens. I'd love to live up there. Do you think it's cold or warm up there?

DELMOUNT. Hmmm. I don't know. Cold maybe? Warm? I don't know.

CARNELLE. (*Looking at herself in the mirror.*) It used to be brown. I had brown hair. Brown.

POPEYE. The man at the observatory he's talking about things such as black holes in space, globular clusters, blue giant stars and other galaxies, he says, "If you can think of it; you've got it." My mind's about to burst just trying.

CARNELLE. (*Looking around the room.*) Grace. Eternal grace. Grace. Hey, hey. I wanna watch the fireworks. (*She picks up the dog and runs out the dressing room ablaze with excitement.*) Hey! Hey, how do I get up there? I wanna come up!

DELMOUNT. (*Overlapping.*) Oh child, you're coming up?!

CARNELLE. Yes! Yes! I wanna come up! I've changed my mind! I'm coming up. How do I get up?!

POPEYE. (*Overlapping.*) Hurray! Hurray! It's easy! You just run around there and jump off of them piled up boxes and climb up the pole!

CARNELLE. Great! I'm on my way! I'm coming up! (*She exits* U.R.)

POPEYE. WOW! She's coming up! I'm so happy! I'm happy!

DELMOUNT. Oh, Popeye! (*He grabs her and kisses her full on the mouth.*) I've been dreaming about you at night. I see you riding across the sea with a host of green whales. Popeye, I love you.

POPEYE. (*Past ecstasy.*) I feel like m'teeth is gonna fall out a my head. (*Carnelle appears on the roof; she is carrying the dog.*)

CARNELLE. Hey! I'm up here! I made it! I'm up.

DELMOUNT. That's right! Now just slide on out here. That's it. Good. You made it.

CARNELLE. Oh, will you look at all those stars in the sky.

POPEYE. Yeah.

DELMOUNT. Oh, yeah.

CARNELLE. Listen, I—I don't know what I was thinking about this afternoon—when I was screaming and all.

DELMOUNT. Please, it's alright. You don't have to say anything. Everythings all right.

CARNELLE. It's just I was upset about not being able to leave

70

in the blaze of glory. Of course, I know it doesn't matter. I mean, the main thing is — well, the main thing is . . . Gosh; I don't know what the main thing is. I don't have the vaguest idea. (*Carnelle is laughing when the first firecracker explodes in the sky.*)

DELMOUNT. Wait! It's started!

POPEYE. (*As gold light floods their faces.*) A gold one! Look, it's a gold one!

CARNELLE. (*Now red light.*) Why, it's bursting into red! Red! Crimson red!

POPEYE. Pow!! Pow! pow. (*And then silently mouthing it.*) Pow. . . . (*The explosion is over. They sit in silence for a moment.*)

CARNELLE. Gosh, it's a nice night.

DELMOUNT. As nice as they come. (*Hold a moment. Blackout.*)

END OF PLAY

PROPERTY PLOT

PROP PRESETS—ACT I:

ONSTAGE:

R. door closed
Plant stand
Potted fern
Hedge
Basket of wool
Spinning wheel (check for no price tag)
Armchair (check for no price tag)
Phone table (check for no price tag)
   phone plugged in
   mug of pencils
   towel
Record player—plugged in
   record on turntable
Record jacket
Photo cube—on top shelf
Rug—secured w/carpet tape
Side table (check for no price tag)
   steno pad
Sofa (check for no price tag)
   2 flags, sticks up & unrolled
   pillow, covering flags
   drill rifle
Desk (check for no price tag)
   blotter on U. edge
   lamp, plugged in
   ashtray, D. corner
   2 sketches, face down
Desk chair, pushed in (check for no price tag)
Wastepaper basket, U. of desk
Benches stacked, covered w/ sheet
Coat rack, half covered w/ sheet

OFFSTAGE:

Shelf:
Wooden spoons (2) and stainless steel knives (2)